Seeking a
WELCOMING SHORE

Seeking a
WELCOMING SHORE

Manuela Durling

SEEKING A WELCOMING SHORE

iUniverse books may be ordered through booksellers or by contacting:

iUniverse
1663 Liberty Drive
Bloomington, IN 47403
www.iuniverse.com
1-800-Authors (1-800-288-4677)

ISBN: 978-1-4917-5727-7 (sc)
ISBN: 978-1-4917-5728-4 (e)

Library of Congress Control Number: 2014922585

Printed in the United States of America.

iUniverse rev. date: 12/27/2014

It is so small a thing,
To have enjoy'd the sun,
To have lived light in the spring,
To have loved, to have thought, to have done.

—Mathew Arnold, "From the Hymn of Empedocles"

CONTENTS

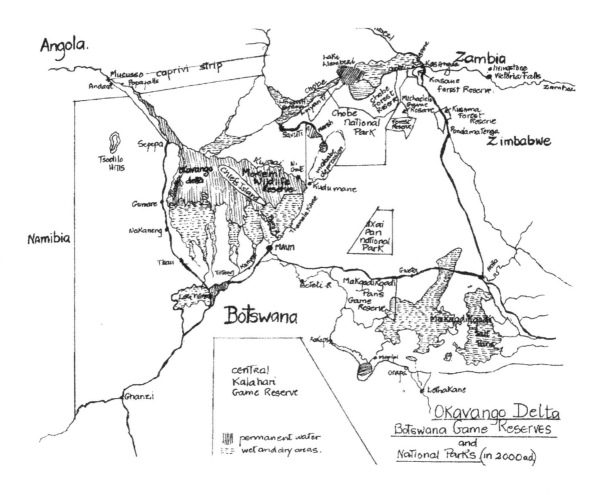

Angola.

Namibia

Mucusso — caprivi strip
Andara Popafalls

Sepepa

Tsodilo
Hills

Gumare

NaKaneng

Tsau

Ghanzi

Botswana

Lake Ngami

Kunya

Toteng

Boteli R.

Kokong

central
Kalahari
Game Reserve

permanent water
wet and dry areas.

Lake
Liambezi

Chobe

Linyanti
swamp

Savuti

Marsh

Chobe
National
Park

Sepopa

Okavango
delta

Chiefs Island

Moremi
Wildlife
Reserve

Kwai
R.

N-
gabe

Moabe
depression

Kudumane

Tamalakane

MAUN

Nxai
Pan
national
Park

Makgadikgadi
Pans
Game Reserve

Makgadikgadi
salt
Pans

Gweta

Nata

Zambia
Livingstone
Victoria Falls
Kasane
Kasane forest Reserve.
Zambezi

Michaelelo
Game
Reserve

Kusane
Forest
Reserve

Forest
Reserve

Pandamatenga

Zimbabwe

Mopipi
Orapa

LothaKane

Okavango Delta
Botswana Game Reserves
and
National Parks (in 2000ad)

PREFACE

It had been a glimmer of hope, an expectation of a brighter future. It had, in some cases, felt more like a sense of desperation and the overwhelming need to go out in the world to explore its possibilities and to shrug off the present circumstance, which, in some measure, propelled many of my relatives to seek lands which they had only heard about, lands about which they knew very little. It had been, to a large extent, the sense of adventure that had moved them to take the chance on a new place, a new continent, and a new way of life. They were driven by the glimmer of high expectations of a new life and almost magical ideas of a prosperous future.

In the case of my parents, they made the decision to leave their homeland and embark on a journey, one that would lead them to a place where the languages spoken were many and varied, where the colour of the inhabitants' skin was vastly different, and where the peoples' customs were primitive and often strange. The land was nonetheless spectacular. The sun shone brightly, and the huge mountain of gold, the largest gold reef in the world, held a promise of endless prosperity.

There was promise of an interesting life ahead, pregnant with possibilities that had not even been imagined in the staid and stuffy land of my parents' ancestors. The family left behind was mired in the daily routines of the middle class. They lived among old battlefields and vast, overwhelming cathedrals that were constant reminders of an old and demanding religion. Theirs was a place where class lines were rigidly maintained and monuments bespoke of battles that had taken place long ago and still cast irreverent shadows on the present. There is no doubt that those who had been born with the proverbial silver spoon would lead rich and rewarding lives and that the abundance of their lifestyles would be hard to duplicate anywhere else. But for the masses of those whose life was only a daily grind for survival, life was hard. They faced the sameness of each day. One's position in society was predicated by fixed rules, and the pattern of lives was set in the stone of old monuments, which reminded them of the intransigence of class and an old religion. The place did not augur well for many of the young people's futures. For the young, leaving home was the best option.

There were only a few places that were regarded as suitable for new immigrants. Brazil was the first that came to mind when Portuguese people thought of leaving home. There was the shiny new country, with its immense forests of the Amazon, its huge landmass, and its minuscule population.

Fortunately, the language spoken was Portuguese. It was the place pregnant with possibilities, where everything grew in the sunshine, sugar cane thrived, and tropical fruits fell from the trees. Even the most inept were unlikely to starve in the midst of such abundance. Brazil also had the civilized area of Rio, which was graced with a monarch for a short period of time before the monarchy was abolished. All this held great appeal for my maternal grandfather, who had been titled and had tarnished his reputation when Portugal became a republic. He had wanted to foment a revolution and, as a result, was asked by the police to accept the alternate to prison: an exile to Brazil. He had no choice, so he took his older daughter and left, literally on the next boat.

I had been brought up in the glory days of South Africa, but I was never a South African, despite having been born there. My parents, Portuguese by birth, had continued to be Portuguese by choice. I, too, had been registered as a Portuguese citizen. There was always the feeling that our stay in Africa was not a permanent one. When life started to deteriorate, when the apartheid laws were promulgated, there seemed to be little choice but to consider emigration. In a way, we still wanted to take in whatever we could of the glorious landscapes of Africa. We decided to fill our days exploring the magnificence of the African landscape and going on safaris to spectacular areas we had not had previously seen. We explored the wild places and mingled with hordes of wild animals, the waterways filled with hippos. We spent our last days in Africa in the most glorious setting of the Okavango Swamp, the largest swamp in the world. This was, indeed, the coup de grâce. We spent more time in this glorious wetland which epitomize all that we loved about the wilds of Africa – more than anywhere else. The memories of those magnificent adventures will stay with us forever and make for interesting reading.

Children who are fortunate enough to have been brought up in a foreign country come, over time, to understand, meld, and make themselves part of the new experience. In my case, assimilation and belonging were never going to be options. Those who have been brought up belonging to a distinct culture, sharing experiences and values with their fellow citizens and enjoying a uniformity of language and style, have a propensity to think similar thoughts and have their world shaped by similar biases and attitudes. For a European transplant to an African country, there is an inbuilt and ever-present alienation in interpreting the world in ways that have no relevance to the present circumstance. It is as if the keys do not fit the doors, behind which mundane objects can be scrutinized. It is like looking through keyholes that do not allow a view of the entire scene, only distorted slices of a skewed reality. I was aware that I was viewing things around me from a perspective very different from that of my parents. They had firmly entrenched middle-class values and continued to interpret the world in light of ancient ideas when faced with a new and very different country: South Africa. For them, there was no experience of dissonance. They merely viewed the new landscapes through ready-made prisms, their values remaining intact.

It had occurred to me that what was an unalterably correct response in one language was not necessarily so in another. Values were not set in stone; they were different from one culture to another. This was a monumental discovery for a very young child, the most valuable lesson of my then short life. It allowed me to meander from one language to another, from one culture to another, without hesitancy, as I knew that the "rules" and explanations of the world around me were not as inflexible as the adults would have me believe. Instead, it was only the shifting sands of cultural perspective. This early recognition of the world around me allowed me to form my own ideas about happenings in my small world and even recognize absurdities.

My father, on the other hand, did not adjust his perspective one iota from the time he landed in Africa to the day he died, nearly forty years later. He accepted all the old myths and values and remained a happy and well-adjusted man. To be buffeted by the different winds of vastly differing perspectives was as valuable a lesson as could be learnt anywhere. It was a soul-expanding experience. I inherited a multicultural point of view and, as I grew, traversed the shark-infested waters of differing cultural values, but I had also learnt my lessons well. My world was a happy place. As I grew older, the turmoil, the dissent, and the apartheid regime all blossomed and cast shadows on the future my parents and I had planned for our lives. There were times when I thought that we might adjust, only to find that the future was too threatening for us even to consider staying. My family members died one by one in the short period before we sailed to a different continent, so the roots we had cherished were all gone in a short period of time. We struggled to readjust our lives without the family I had cherished. The political situation deteriorating by the day, we became accustomed to the idea of leaving. After the shooting at Sharpville, our minds were irrevocably made up. We were convinced that we had chosen the only feasible option.

$$*\quad*\quad*$$

When married with a family, we carefully examined several alternatives, especially when the situation in South Africa became untenable. We knew that leaving was not an option; it was a necessity. We had not embarked on the decision lightly. Too many dark episodes brought about our appraisal of the reality in which we lived. Because of the way things were going, it became apparent that, sooner or later, we all might just be killed. Leaving was foremost in our daily thoughts. The traumas of everyday life convinced us that the quicker we left, the better for everyone. It was a distinct moment, deciding that I could not go on in the land of my birth. Not only was my life at risk, but also my children's lives were at risk. I could see no future ahead for my family.

We cast about for ideas and finally decided that we would leave Africa and head to the land down under. There were travels; there was exploration. We considered the possibilities and then finally made the move to a land which I had never considered as a possibility. It was too cold, too snowy, and too far north. Yet there we were, most of our dreams fulfilled. We had found our home at long last. It has been a long road for various members of my immediate family, and a pleasant road for my maternal grandfather, the first to leave the motherland. He was able to land on his feet, continue enjoying the status of minor royalty, and continue his extravagant way of life in Brazil.

For my parents, who opted for another continent, Africa, life was hard. They were weighed down with the responsibilities of representing the Portuguese State and took life very seriously, with little time to enjoy the fruits of their labours. They were imbued with a stern sense of duty, conscious that, although they were in a new and beautiful land, they had, in fact, imported all the trials, tribulations, and mores of the land left behind. With them, it was as if the new life was somehow superimposed on the old. They had dragged along the old land of their forebears, which cast a long shadow on their new existence. They saw no need to change. In fact, their jobs dictated that they stay in a fixed niche, promulgating the way of life that they had left behind, but just in another city and on a distant continent.

I, who had been born in the new country and knew no other, found that it was a difficult proposition to navigate between the new landscape of a different culture and the traditional way of life demanded by my family. Before we had an opportunity to consider leaving this land enmeshed in turmoil, we were cast into distressing episodes during our daily lives. The brutality of the lives of the indigenous population, the predatory manifestations of the police, and the incidents that ensued, in which we were physically attacked, were all around us. Plus, the farm we were living on was set alight, endangering our very existence.

Leaving was more easily said than done. We were on the verge of casting ourselves from the continent when we lost family members. With every illness and subsequent death, we postponed our leaving, going instead to the cemetery to mourn the family members who had fallen by the wayside and would not be able to come with us on our proposed exodus to a new and more peaceful land.

Then there was the second generation, who, having decided to cast their fate on the troubled waters of old regimes, suddenly found that life was too dangerous in Mozambique, East Africa, for them to contemplate staying in the region. Like my daughter, they were hustled out of settled lives in the middle of a revolution, only to battle their way to join older members of the family on the far continents where they had chosen to start new and safer lives.

It was a tumultuous exodus. It took several years and many false starts. Certainly, the older members of my family had given moving serious consideration. Those coming from the motherland sampled and explored several countries before casting them aside as wanting. It was not an entirely negative experience. It was a joyful seeking of possibilities on various continents and sampling differing ways of life, and eventually finding what was finally and unequivocally the right fit. It was also a decision to go to places where there were no other family members and where the culture was new, open, and accepting. In time, my family members appreciated these new countries. Those who settled in them, realizing that they had made good decisions, would never have considered going back to the lands from whence they had come. They were in their chosen lands to stay, probably forever.

This, then, is a story of many lands and various members of an extended family who sought and found new habitations and new ways of life, either by choice or after being forced by exigent circumstance. It was the story of events that made staying in the land of their birth no longer possible. It was heartache; it was adventure; it was akin to plunging into the void. It was, in fact, seeking a welcoming shore and, in certain cases, being lucky enough to find it.

Before the final leave-taking, there was a period of reflection. We enumerated all the places that we should revisit, and we said goodbye to the areas we had loved so much in the past. We gathered our thoughts together and went off to say farewell to places that had cast shadows on our souls, with the knowledge that we would never see them again. One area in particular had left us beguiled. Tom, my husband, made arrangements to revisit the Okavango Swamp and Botswana. He was waiting for my school holidays, but he only told me of his plans at the last moment. I went along with mixed feelings. Looking back now, I can say that this adventure was probably the most exciting of all our African adventures and the one that left indelible memories. It was there that we said our final farewells to Africa.

WEST OF THE SUN AND EAST OF THE MOON – THE OKAVANGO SWAMP OF THE KALAHARI

The Okavango Swamp is the largest swamp in the world. The astronauts saw it from space as a large triangular scar just below the African equator. Here, the land is shaken by enormous earthquakes, which reshape the surface so that it is never the same. The area's lakes and rivers are built on a fragile infrastructure. In fact, the swamp has no water of its own. In the dry summer months, the waters burst forth from the mountains in the highlands of Angola and fill this desert land with borrowed water, not only to inundate the swamp but also to transverse the land southwards to fill Lake Ngami in the west and the Makgadikgadi Salt Pans in the east.

Earthquakes constantly rumble beneath the surface. Some are so violent that they have been detected as far afield as the Seismological Laboratory in California where, in 1952, as many as twenty-three earthquakes were recorded.

When the earth is at the driest and all is parched in the Kalahari, which is the moment the waters arrive after their long journey from the mountains in Angola. In the summer, the waters trickle and then swell to fill the Okavango Basin for the winter season. When the land itself is dry and there is no rainfall is when the Angolan bounty refreshes and rejuvenates the land to the south, bringing it to life. The change is spectacular. All of a sudden, birdlife increases to the millions, and wildlife by the thousands. The land is supported and nurtured. It is only the anomaly of the waters coming from the north that creates the illusion of lushness in what is basically a desert.

Suddenly, after the rains in the north, huge swells break over the swamp. Rivers, channels, lakes, lagoons, and channels spill into an area which is over fifteen thousand square kilometres wide. Perversely, when the local rainfall ceases, the Okavango is at its most resplendent.

There are no set paths, channels, or even fixed roads in the swamp. These alter year to year, depending on the caprice of the water flow. Nothing is predictable, not even the whereabouts of the huge herds that roam this incredible land and call it home. Small roads run on the periphery of the Okavango, and small villages are to be found dotted here and there on the edges of the waterways.

The swamp breaks up into smaller and smaller channels as it dissipates in the Kalahari sands and travels south to form Lake Ngami. This lake varies in size and complexity from year to year.

Its water supply is uncertain and alternates between being a huge watery haven where swarms of quelea are so high in number that they resemble plagues of locusts to resembling nothing more than a muddy depression, which it does in certain years.

Lake Ngami was talked about in Victorian living rooms for the profusion of birdlife and animals it supported.

It was in 1750 that the Yabei tribe moved into the area, but it was in 1849 that David Livingstone walked into this riverscape, being the first white man to reach Okavango's shores. He reported in his journals that it was indeed "a fine stretch of water." The Batawana tribe that moved its cattle into this bountiful area and built its huts on the shores of the lake.

Reports of the extraordinary bounty offered by Lake Ngami reached far afield, at which time hunters pounced on this area and proceeded in very short order to slaughter twelve thousand elephants in an orgy of death.

Then, gradually, amidst all this bounty, the lake began to change. The reed boats that the Africans had used to transport themselves through the swamps were, over time, left abandoned in the waterways of the Okavango. These reeds of papyrus had sprouted once again and had grown to cause massive blockages, which altered the flow of the water channels. The river choked to death and so did the channels flowing southwards into Lake Ngami.

The lake was dying a slow death because of the blockage. As the waters receded, the fish were stranded in the ensuing shallows. Birds descended by the millions to gorge themselves in the feast of a lifetime. Huge flocks of geese, pelicans, fish eagles, herons, cranes, gulls, pink flamingoes, and waterhens attacked and ate the dying fish.

Then a drought ensued. The cattle were stranded, as they needed water every day to survive. As the lake was no longer being fed by the Okavango, it deteriorated and became but a few puddles and mud. These were the very conditions that favoured the breeding of the mosquitoes, which had a heyday, growing into huge clouds and settling on all the inhabitants of the area. By the thousands, Africans died of cerebral malaria. To add to the sudden misery, rinderpest (foot and mouth disease) came to the already struggling cattle and wiped them out. The locals who had survived this calamity planted crops to sustain themselves only to find that as soon as the crops were ready for harvest, quelea ate them. These arrived by the thousands, demolishing the food source.

The Tabawanans were to remember 1896 as the year this fertile lake vanished. The lake was abandoned, as it was now a place of horror and death. For many years thereafter, the lake was deserted.

In 1953, the lake was resuscitated by the slow trickle of the water that had managed to escape the blockages in the swamp and form new channels towards the south. At first, small swirls were reported in the shallows of the lake. More water followed. Suddenly, one could hear the screeching of birds that had come back. Fish swam down the Okavango and into the new lake, but few could survive in the murky waters. Most died. But bream and barbel not only survived but also flourished.

At first, the lake looked like green pea soup. It was ugly and smelly, but it was gradually filled with more clean water from the Okavango channels so that the birds were back in the thousands, the quelea swarming in clouds. In fact, there are so many quelea that when they flew and alighted in small trees, the branches broke under the sheer weight of their numbers.

I saw the lake after its revival and was astonished at the birdlife. It must be remembered that birds are not invested in living near the lake; they can fly off if there is another calamity. They are opportunistic, exploiting the good times and flying away in the bad. But the sad news is that the tribal people were lured back to the shining waters, bringing their cattle and keeping them in little enclosures that have an air of permanence about them. Once more, the ecology is being altered by the presence of cattle. Villages are springing up. The lessons of the last two hundred years have not been learnt. This lake is a mirage, teetering on the verge of another extinction.

There are two geologic fault lines that control the way the water flows through to the Kalahari Basin. The Gomare fault is a continuation of the Great Rift Valley. The flow of the water is blocked by two southern faults: the Kunyere and the Thamalakane. The latter, like a dam, redirects the waters and sends them in a change of direction eastwards through a break in the fault to form one river – the Botetli. I came to know the Thamalakane well during my stay at Bobby Wilmot's camp, which was located in this area.

EAST OF THE SUN AND WEST OF THE MOON – SAFARI TO THE OKAVANGO SWAMPS AND THE N'GAMILAND NATURE RESERVE

It was August 1962 when my husband Tom and I went on safari to the Okavango Swamps in what was then Northern Bechuanaland and is now Botswana. We left shortly after midnight in two vehicles, a Land Rover and an International heavy-duty truck, both four-wheelers heavily loaded with seventeen people, bags, baggage, tents, sleeping gear, guns, maps, food, and four barrels of petrol which were destined to be used later in the motorboats in the swamps.

From Johannesburg, we proceeded westwards through the Northern Transvaal on roads that were sheer bliss compared to those which we were to encounter later. The road ran through Palapye leading to Francistown, where there was only a small population of Europeans in a sea of Botswanans. There, taking a detour through a vast expanse of flat veld, we saw many limp and bedraggled ostriches, their feathers, in a sad state of repair, dragging on the ground. Unless properly cared for with constant spraying against the depredations of lice and other vermin plus a strict regimen of vitamins, the majestic plumes deteriorate into the ragged and dirty grey and black covering found on the birds in their wild state.

The vegetation is sparse, but here and there are well-marked clusters of palms (*Hyphaene*), which are a notable feature of the area. The stems, thinly dispersed, are thicker in the middle than at the base. A cluster of these palms, all minus their feathery-looking "tops," grow like masts above the lower vegetation. The wood has an attractive speckled grain and is intensely hard. This species attains a great age. The fruits are the size of tennis balls and, in famine years, are eaten by Africans. However, the taste of this fruit is like sugary sawdust. Only a highly specialized digestive tract could possibly be induced to cope with it.

The Makgadikgadi Salt Pan, that vast depression on the edge of the Kalahari Desert, thirstily absorbs the waters of the Nata, the Botetli, and other rivers which traverse the Okavango Swamp. They start off with a roar and end in the whimper of a salt pan in the Kalahari Desert.

When I was there, the surrounding land was covered in luxuriant grass, and, after the rain, smiling flowers burst into radiant bloom, transforming the scene of naked sunbaked earth into a verdant haven. It is the Botetli River that empties into the salt pan. The Botelti is a magnificent river, with large trees and mimosa bushes on its banks, margins of reeds, large crocodiles, and endless clamorous flocks of birds. It is this river that brings the last of the Okavango waters, sometimes reduced to only a trickle, out across the desert. Without it, no life could be sustained in these Kalahari sands. This riverbank, at first, was the only "road" into the swamp, one which provided good hunting, as thousands of herds came to drink from its banks.

Years ago, local tribes brought their cattle to the banks of this river and decided to settle in this location. Once the water had been two metres deep, but now it is a mere twelve-hundred-mile skeleton. The Okavango had, in Victorian times, been larger than Lake Victoria.

When it rains, shallow pans still form. Birds come by the thousands to the shallow blue pans, creating a huge spectacle on this temporary lake. There was a time not so long ago when two hundred and fifty thousand wildebeest roamed in this area. Then, just as suddenly as the water retreated, the grasses no longer grew and the animals died. Next, fires erupted and the grasses burnt. The herds were once more decimated as the food source disappeared.

Grasses eventually grew back, painfully, but this was a fragile crop. The ecology was altered by the intense grazing of the local cattle. The land could not sustain the abuse. The grasses gradually gave way to annuals and then weeds. Today, the only thing that remains is thorn bush.

Later, springhares began to assert their claim on this land. They once bred in the millions and provided meat for the taking. Suddenly, foot and mouth disease arrived in waves and destroyed all the cattle in the region. The area was once more devastated. The cow – a foreign invader and mighty destroyer – was named the most deadly animal in the region.

To camp on the shores of the pan is to experience a symphony of frog-like sounds. The cacophony includes the incessant shrill notes of cicadas, crickets, and grasshoppers, which merge with the vigorous basso- profundo vocalizations of the large frogs. One notices the deep, organ-like bass of the great bullfrogs and the shrill piping "piet, piet" sounds of the little tree frogs, which are their climbing cousins.

Beneath the salty crust of the innocent earth around the pans, the sticky yellow clay of quicksand is a feature to inspire dread. Large flocks of marabou storks live in this area. With their humped backs, bald pates, and ponderous bills, they are certainly quaint fellows. The ubiquitous "rain hawks" gather here, too, and live in this area, no doubt attracted to the abundance of mopani caterpillars found in the clusters of mopani bushes a little east of the pan. A recent mass invasion of caterpillars attracted a great influx of birdlife: stately pink flamingoes, blue-grey herons, the shy little night heron, ibises, darters, blacksmith plovers, snipe, collared sandpipers, snowy egrets, and lively avocets. Duck, teal, and divers are to be found shovelling in the mud of the still pools they love, and white-headed fish eagles with their cheery ringing scream are common.

We drove onwards to Nata, a picturesque little African village on the banks of the Nata River. I abandoned my lunch to intrude on the headmaster of the local school. He was a sincere young man who was attempting, against all odds, to educate the children of this remote village. Nata has only one bus stop, no trains, and one semi-dry river where the donkeys and local cattle water unceremoniously next to the tribal woman filling her water containers with the murky water. Making tea with the local water prompted the question, "Will you have yours with or without dung?"

Against this background or, rather, the lack thereof, a young headmaster struggles against poverty, hunger, and ignorance without electricity, with classes of over fifty children, and with little or no equipment.

I was invited to attend the ongoing classes when I explained that I was a teacher. The headmaster taught reading with books sent from England extolling the joys of English trains, Thames steamships, Brighton Beach, the funfair at Blackpool, and other strange things experienced by the people of very ordinary English households. It occurred to me that, to the Nata schoolchildren, this was tantamount to our schools' teaching our children about the daily lives of the Martians on Mars. Our most commonplace experiences are totally outside the ken of these children. Their English readers only reflect brief imaginings in some flight of fancy.

At the school, prizes – packages of seeds imported from South Africa – were awarded for first place in a number of subjects. The rewards were then watered, tenderly tended, and guarded from the scorching sun and predators. They produced mystical crops of lettuce and tomatoes and other extraordinary edible delights. I was intrigued by this school and the intensity and passion with which these children in their overcrowded classrooms wanted so desperately to learn.

After Nata, the road is closed to all but four-wheel vehicles, mainly large Albion trucks. The road consists of sand three to four feet thick, which makes it very heavy going. While our cars groaned beneath their loads, the wheels spun furiously, attempting for hours to drive 273 miles. The passengers climbed endlessly in and out of the vehicles and pushed and sweated, and the cars tilted precariously at 45 degree angles.

Too tired to speak, we tumbled into Bobby Wilmot's base camp outside of the capital, Maun, on the Thamalakane River near the Botetli. This river is one of the main streams that come out from the Okavango Swamp at its base.

By the time we arrived, the insufferable heat had turned into cold. This, we were to learn, was characteristic of African deserts.

We had indifferent tents and equipment, and, as a result, the cold came up through the flimsy sleeping bags. It was impossible to sleep, as the beds were raised about six inches from the ground and allowed the cold to penetrate. We shuffled around the camp, begging for newspapers in order to insulate our beds a little bit.

The swamps, which to the uninitiated conjure up visions of mud and mangroves, were really quite different. The Okavango swamps were, in reality, nine hundred square miles of crystal-clear waterways interspersed with islands, all teeming with game. We had arrived at Bobby's base camp on the Botetli River and had no idea at first that the mighty Okavango was so close at hand.

The camp was well organized. Tom and I had a tent under the mopani trees, which grew in clusters everywhere on the banks of the Botelti. These trees were home to the tsetse fly. The mosquitoes swarmed in the millions as soon as it became dark. Cerebral malaria exists in the swamps. We took quinine derivatives every day in an attempt to stave off any sickness. I had had malaria as a child in Mozambique, so I was more aware than most of the predations of the disease. During the day, the tsetse flies find that it is too hot to cling to the leaves of the mopani trees. They creep out, searching for warm blood on which to feed.

These flies were unlike any I had seen previously. They did not fit into my concept of how a fly should be or behave. For starters, they were very large as flies go, up to three quarters of an inch in size and of a dull greyish colouration. Their outstanding characteristic, in my view, is that they are languid. They find a moving object, an animal or, in our case, clothing, and then settle down to hitch a ride. They do not like to fly any distances, preferring a free ride. I saw quite a few men in the camp with their shirt backs full of flies hitching a ride in comfort. These flies refuse to be shaken off. It is in this fashion that they are disseminated from one area to another.

At that time, border posts were set up, not so much as to check travellers' papers as to check on the deadly flies. Small buildings were staffed by serious African guards all equipped, not with guns, but with sticks with swatters on the ends. These were wielded with precision movements under cars and around travellers so as to dislodge any flies attempting to hitch rides. After the swatting, these guards stood in a line and saluted before they marched off into the shade of their post. They took their duties very seriously. We tried not to laugh at their emotive performance.

Where *Gossina morsitans,* the mopani tree, grows, so do the flies breed. These tsetse flies do not lay eggs. They are viviparous, the first stage of their development taking place within the parent's body. The fecundity of this fly is, fortunately, in no way comparable to that of other fly species which produce bunches of eggs, but it is curious to note that when pregnant, these flies eject their young if pressure is placed on the abdomen. In the shade, in hollowed-out tree stumps or in tree trunks, many oval black glossless pupae are to be found. They are easily recognized by the two tiny projections at one end. The larvae are less readily found. They are whitish in colour when freshly deposited, and fatter than in the pupal stage.

Our knowledge of the natural enemies of the fly is still hazy. But this is the way that the science is going. If some control could be found, then millions of fauna would be saved, as well as the lives of the African population that persists in living in these deadly areas.

Earlier, attempts were made to clear the areas of the tsetse fly by using Dieldrin soon after it was first produced. Today, aircraft spray Endosulfan in an attempt to control the fly, but the vastness of the area makes the idea almost untenable. Maun, at least, has been made fly-free in more recent times. It has become clear that the wildlife can share space and coexist with the fly, but humankind cannot.

Everywhere are enormous anthills. There are twenty species of termites recorded in the area and in the swamps. One species produces an eight-foot tower.

There are huge swarms of bees roaming through the veld and the swamps. Long ago, seekers of black honey proliferated here. Africans would come great distances to go into the swamp and its remoter areas to collect the enormous amounts of wild black honey, freely available for the taking. These men were known as the hive tappers. They returned not only with the honey but also with the deadly sleeping sickness. The tsetse was everywhere in the Okavango. At first, the Africans did not understand the connection between the fly and the honey and thought that the disease come directly from the honey. Today, they understand the connection. Still, the intrepid try their luck at collecting the black swamp honey, often at a terrible cost.

After a couple of days acclimatizing ourselves to Bobby Wilmot's camp, we were anxious to proceed north for our fist glimpses of other areas of the Okavango Swamp. We got back into our trucks and proceeded towards the River Kwai area.

We passed a few camps that had luxurious equipment, beds with sheets, and bedside tables with kerosene lamps. These camps were hives of activity. They catered exclusively to Americans who had come to shoot "the big ones." These camps were, we were told, very expensive, but they were set up for people who did not spend their days amidst the usual circumstances associated with bush living. Campers here enjoyed four-course meals, access to collections of prize rifles, cocktails at sunset, and a motley collection of African servants in khaki uniforms (who looked uncomfortable and a little out of place with their new clothes), who were there as trackers and helpers to smooth the ruffles of the rich, all the way. There, too, were six brand new Land Rovers gleaming in the sunlight, awaiting the forays into areas where the clients were initiated in the so-called sport of hunting, which I call uncompromising slaughter.

On our first night away from Bobby's base camp in the northern part of the Okavango Swamp, we built a fire and placed the beds we had brought along in a ring around it. We slept out under the stars. It was glorious to view the unobstructed stars and to feel the primordial stillness of the night; but it was quite intimidating to awake from sleep to the roaring of lion. In the still of the night, the sounds carry great distances. To me, it seemed as if the roars came from the adjacent trees. Here, in this area, Africa is herself, unspoiled from the encroachments of humanity. While we slept, animals walked through our gathering. In the morning, Bobby tried to identify the spoor. It seemed as if we had been visited by a family of hyenas. To the left of the camp near the area where the vehicles were parked, there was indeed the spoor of lion.

None of this was quite as unsettling as the screeches of the baboons. They gave frantic piercing screams which were spine-chilling as they sounded alarms among the groves of giant acacia trees, which they favoured as their sleeping places.

Scampering around were the ugliest of nature's children – the warthogs. When they encountered us, they turned tail, but they had the droll habit of trotting along with one eye looking at us from over their backs. Still, they suffered no loss of dignity and, at the same time, kept their plumed top tails strictly erect.

This area was filled with civets, lions, leopards, cheetahs, caracals, servals, and black-footed wildcats, all of the family *Felidae,* which in N'gamiland is particularly well represented. The dog tribe, too, was much in evidence, as well as both species of hyena, some jackals, and two species of fox.

The area of the Kwaai is in the heart of the Okavango Swamp. We were surrounded by water. In front of our small camp were enormous stretches of papyrus-fringed canals. Along one side of the camp was a large lagoon completely covered in large lotus-like leaves, from which pink flowers raised their delicate blooms which swayed in the breeze.

Bobby was very familiar with the area. He had been shooting crocodile on the Kwaai for many years. On our second night in our new camp, Bobby organized a crocodile hunt for those who felt up to it. Being the adventurous sort, I was certainly game. At dusk, we set off along the main stream near our camp. The swamp felt ethereal in the glow of the setting sun. There were five boats filled with our fellow campers and the croc crew, and one larger boat with Bobby and the women of the group.

We sailed by colonies of white herons sleepily nesting in the shallows, gazing unafraid at our intruding boats. Bobby sat in a small deckchair in the prow of the leading boat, wrapped in a white blanket and wielding a powerful handheld torch, with which he scanned the shallows as we went chugging along. Two beady eyes reflected back at us; like the taillights of a small car on a dark night, they told of the lurking menace in the papyrus shallows. Crocodiles are fearless and regard anything on or in the water as potential prey. Unblinkingly, they awaited the approaching boat, while Bobby, still shining the light which he held in one hand, aimed a heavy-calibre rifle with deadly accuracy at one of the beasts. After the shot resounded in the night, long poles with hooks on the ends hauled the crocodile aboard. The African crew then severed the crocodile's spinal cord in haste. This has become standard practice, as it has happened that some crocodiles, momentarily stunned by a bullet, resuscitated. The hunters, in such a circumstance, have been known to beat a hasty and undignified retreat into the water, leaving the croc beating about angrily in the bottom of the empty boat.

The impenetrableness of the swamps, their general inaccessibility, keeps the crocs from being completely shot out. But they also provide a source of revenue for the intrepid. Cattle cannot readily be kept in this area. What cattle do exist are infected with rinderpest, one of the ravages of the tsetse fly.

The seven crocs caught that night were brought back to land and carefully skinned. The underbellies were then rolled in salt. In this state, the skins are sent to France to be cured. In a raw state, in those days, they could bring about ten pounds. After they are cured, they brought eight times that price.(1960).

Bobby explained that it was illegal to shoot crocodiles that were under four feet in length; a penalty of four pounds sterling was levied as a fine if a "baby" was shot.

We spent five hours gliding silently along the canals of the swamp in the moonlight. It was a totally alien scenario. Sometimes, there was an unearthly silence in our boat, while surrounding us there were the sounds of frogs, cicadas, and the occasional bird which chirped when our presence disturbed it. We did not talk. We just glided along in the eerie moonlight, never knowing what might appear around the next bend in the swampy channel. I felt, like Alice, that I had fallen down a rabbit hole. Despite the numbers in our group and the vast differences in background and nationality, we were all struck silent by the awesome beauty of the night, making a visceral connection to the wild.

It was well after midnight when Bobby, who had allowed us to see a small piece of his amazing world, suddenly laid aside the blanket covering his knees and leapt out of the boat and into the shallows. Knee-deep in the water and barehanded, he plunged into the water with suddenness and brought up a baby crocodile, which came aboard complaining bitterly with fierce squirming, tail lashings, and baby cries of protest. He sounded very much like a small child throwing a tantrum. His mouth was held tightly shut until a small piece of wood was offered to him as a teething ring, of sorts. Once some surgical tape was bound over his mouth, he lay quiet but defiant on the bottom of the boat, all the way back to our campsite on the Kwaai.

Once shut, a baby crocodile's mouth, like its parents', is impossible to prize open without breaking some of its teeth. The "baby" our group had caught was placed in a box. That night, one of the group, a very frightened young man from Zurich who was totally out of his milieu and mostly terrified of everything around him, found his sleeping bag occupied by our baby croc. It was a terrible thing to do. We thought that the poor youth was about to have a heart attack when, after sliding into his sleeping bag, he encountered the cold scaly body of our baby reptile!

It had been a long night!

The following evening, I arranged to get a field bath. A small tent was set up with a canvas bath into which tepid water was poured for washing. Although we were surrounded by water, it was, of course, far too dangerous to try and wash in the shallows. I had got into the bath tent, which was situated a little away from the fire around which most of the group were sitting, enjoying the after-dinner coffee. I had got to the stage where I had taken off all my clothes and was about to enter the bath. I decided instead that I should first try to get behind the tent and into the bushes. There was nobody about. I stepped out gingerly and went behind the tent. Then, in the dark, I tripped on a line attached to a tent peg and fell heavily on a small cardboard box that had been stashed there. Out popped the baby croc. He looked more surprised than I did, but I did give a yelp of fright. Several people came running in my direction only to find me, in the raw, more or less composed and laughing my head off …

We settled into Bobby's camp, which was a daily adventure in itself. I made friends with Cookie. He was a small man with a heavily scarred chest. His left arm looked as if it had poor function. Nevertheless, I discovered that he took off after lunch to fish for bream. I persuaded him to let me go with him. Tiger fish abound in the Botetli, and I caught thirteen bream in very little time. These were roasted on an open fire for dinner and were positively scrumptious.

The evening sounds of the swamp are like some discordant cacophony, but with the silvery light on the water casting pink shadows on the bush, the atmosphere became fairylike.

Every day with Bobby Wilmot was an unabashed adventure. Our boat trips upstream revealed large floating islands of papyrus, reeds, water lilies, and large masses of pink and mauve on shimmering waters. The bird life was so rich and diverse that this area would be a birdwatchers' paradise. The birds have never been systematically categorized or categorized by ornithologists. Many of them bear only local names.

Acres of water lilies formed the most immediate impression. Among these was a very large-leafed species that I had never seen or heard of and that had distinct similarities to the species found in the Brazilian Amazon. Blooms were almost a foot across and differed somewhat from the funnel-shaped calyces of the more common types. With rounded tips inclining slightly forward and snowy white petals framing a golden heart, they formed bowl-shaped blooms of incredible beauty. I pulled up a stem and found that it was at least fifteen feet in length. I also found the more common mauve, purple, and pink varieties of water lily. They bloomed in great masses, and their sweet perfume suffused the air. I also found several species of pygmy lilies, also incredibly beautiful and delicate, but these flourished only in backwater areas with little traffic.

On the shore next to the camp were a number of mokoros, the local boats. An elderly African at the camp informed me that it would normally take a year or so to make one of these craft, but there had been a time when it was possible to buy a mokoro for five pounds. The tree used to build them, *Diospyros mespiliformis,* is called mokokchong locally. *Lonchocarpus capassa* was also used. Neither of these woods is hard or liable to crack, but the latter, which rarely grows straight or attains great size, has a fibrous grain that is difficult to work. Some of the mokoros are made from *Pterocarpus angolensis,* which is indeed a beautiful timber. It is also known as kiaat. The problem with this wood is that the outer few inches of sapwood are likely to flake off from the golden heart. Paddles, however, are frequently made from this wood, and are from five to ten feet long. Punters standing astern can use them to propel the crafts at a considerable rate on a perfectly straight course. Paddles used for punting have a forked end, average fourteen feet in length, and are called n'kashis.

When the Yabei tribe first wandered into the Okavango long ago, they preferred reed boats with long ropes attached. The ropes allowed them to secure the boat for the night when they needed to sleep. The boats could travel great distances downstream with the drift of the waters, and no paddles were needed. The problem was that when the owners of such craft reached their destinations, they abandoned their transportation in the streams, where the boats promptly regrew roots and continued to flourish as papyrus beds!

I witnessed people travelling on the river. They greeted one another with "Dumela" and customarily exchanged local gossip.

While we lived in Bobby Wilmot's camp, I often took the opportunity to explore the waterways, with the excuse that I was going fishing. But it occurred to me that if anything happened to my trusted guide, Cookie, I would have absolutely no way of finding my way home. We took twists and turns and ended up in swift-running channels or small still waters, and it was impossible to recognize any places as places previously visited. Apart from my general ignorance of the channels, the fact that these changed from day to day, depending on the flow of the water, left me in a state of confusion. Islands that were full of game one day might be totally submerged the next, so that my usual ability to recognize landmarks was made useless. It was only when we were on the home stretch that I began to find landmarks and could recognize the part of the river immediately in front of the camp. I usually have a very good sense of direction, but in the swamps I felt totally inadequate. I didn't recognize any landmarks and was not astute enough to distinguish one tree from another as we went by. One patch of papyrus was intrinsically like another. Points on a compass were confusing, too, as I felt we were often travelling in circles as the canals took us along. The compass points did not provide any reference for more than a few yards, at best. I felt that I was negotiating some devilish maze and that my perceptions of reality were not to be trusted.

Substantial-looking islands were, in reality, floating in the waters and moved according to the currents. These islands were often made of sedge, reed, and papyrus, the roots of which had become entwined and tightly interlaced. They might have provided some purchase for wind-driven soil, and then some small aquatic plants could take root and thrive. The surface was exceedingly deceptive. There was no way to stand on one of these seemingly solid islands. Its fragility would cause breaks to appear, and then anything of any weight atop it would plunge into ten feet of water, the tangle of roots and fibres below making it impossible to extricate oneself without a good deal of external help. There is nothing to hang onto or to use in levering a person up. Death by drowning comes quickly. Worse, one in this situation may be attacked by the ever-vigilant crocodiles.

I have seen lovely islands heave and ripple from the currents that were carrying them along. These islands are not to be trusted, as they are havens for leeches.

Here and there, we found cylindrical fish traps. The entry holes were small, but the fish, once caught, were unable to find their way out.

The waterways continued to be unpredictable, filled with papyrus reeds and the dangerous Okavango hippo. We saw "hippo canals" – clearings a few feet wide made by the heavy bodies of the hippos as they swam through the papyrus reeds on their way from one lake to another. These form dangerous waterways. One evening over an open fire, Bobby disclosed the disastrous details that had nearly led to the death of Cookie (our cook and my friendly guide and fishing companion).

As was Bobby's custom, he split his workers into two tribes. One he would leave behind to labour on the skinning and salting of the crocodile skins from the night before. The other he would take with him on forays into the swamps for a night of crocodile fishing. At the time, Bobby had a fairly large boat, certainly much larger than most of the craft found in these waters. It accommodated Bobby, his crew, and paraphernalia for the night's croc-catching activities. As he often did, he cut corners rather than negotiating longish routes around the islands. He decided to cut through the hippo canals. They were wonderful shortcuts and easy for the boat to push through. He had done this a thousand times before and thought nothing of doing it again.

On this particular occasion, however – and horror of horrors – he found a full-size male hippo coming to meet him, head-on. Let me add that hippos are notorious for their forward charge, but when they encounter an obstacle, they are unable to conceive of the notion of going back to whence they had come. The hippo was angry because something was blocking his way and usurping his canal. He charged at Bobby's boat, opened his enormous jaws, and promptly took a bite out of the watercraft.

The boat began to sink. Bobby tried to salvage anything he could from the sinking vessel as it was being chewed to matchsticks. Unfortunately for Cookie, he, like the people of the Okavango, did not know how to swim, for very obvious reasons. He fell headfirst into the water. Bobby threw himself after Cookie, but the hippo got to him first. Its huge jaws clamped onto Cookie's chest and right arm as Cookie frantically tried to get away and onto the impossible papyrus. Bobby bravely pulled him onto a portion of the boat that had finally come to rest on the papyrus. There was blood everywhere. Bobby knew that they were all in serious trouble. Nobody at the camp could come to the rescue, for nobody knew the location of the hunters that night. Had they known, they still might have not get there in time to save the occupants of the wrecked boat from disaster. Bobby did what he could for the desperate Cookie, who had an enormous flap of skin taken from his chest so that his ribs were showing. His right arm was mangled. Bobby rescued his only medicine – some liquor – and kept giving Cookie more and more brandy, until he passed out in an alcohol-induced blur from the severity of his injuries.

Bobby and his gang were on the reeds and in the splintered boat for six hours before a crew in a passing mokoro found them. Some of that crew went for help while others picked up the pieces. Bobby threw Cookie into his truck and made for Maun. There, Cookie was picked up and flown out to Bulawayo in what was then Rhodesia (and is now Zimbabwe) for urgent medical attention. Cookie was saved, miraculously, and returned six months later to work for Bobby. As he had some cooking skills, Bobby made sure that he was employed in that capacity. He never took him out night hunting again.

But Bobby had learnt his lesson well. Wooden boats cannot be taken into the swamps in areas where there are hippo. Steel-bottom boats are the only solution for those who wish to traverse the hippo canals with impunity. It was a financial setback for Bobby, as steel-bottom boats are not only hard to come by but are also terribly expensive. He special-ordered one and never went into a hippo canal again without it.

The local tribes often set fire to the papyrus, and one can smell the fire from miles away. But hardly a dent is made on the papyrus, which appears to be indestructible.

The abundance and diversity of the birdlife was overwhelming. I saw ibis nests, their clutches of eggs neatly laid on the papyrus. Nesting marabou storks were to be seen sleeping curled up on the reeds. They seemed unafraid. After looking at us, they sleepily shut their eyes again, as if we were merely an inconvenience, and then promptly tucked their heads under their wings and went back to sleep.

* * *

After our days at the camp, we were anxious to travel further and proceed north for more glimpses of the Okavango. We encountered more safari camps which were hives of activity. The occupants had been told that here they would be easily able to shoot "the big ones."

All the way, we saw herds of buck grazing. We finally saw a herd of elephants towards sunset.

Bobby Wilmot had planned to have us escorted into the plains surrounding the Kwaai area in order to see for ourselves the vastness of the landscape as well as the thunderous herds that grazed, galloped, and played in the area. Tom, always heavily weighed down with all his cameras and equipment, led the band and followed Kweri, our leader and tracker.

Kweri was a River Bushman, small in stature but said to have the heart of a lion. He was the chief of the local River Bushmen tribe, among whom we had set up camp. Armed only with a knife, he had gone out as a lad of fourteen to avenge the death of his mother, who had been eaten by a lion. He had tracked the lion relentlessly and, over time, had learnt its habits. One day while the lion was sleeping, Kweri plunged his knife into its heart and killed it. He then proceeded to disembowel it. In the entrails, he found some beads that had belonged to his mother.

We roamed stealthily, led by Kweri, in single file through the bush. We saw hoofed animals in alarming numbers. From a distance, they looked like a mirage.

Tom and I walked single file through the bush behind Kweri. Armed with a rusty rifle and moving silently, Kweri showed us the way. He knew the territory intimately. Tom was, as always, heavily laden with cameras. I walked behind him at a leisurely pace. We walked mostly in awed silence, coming suddenly upon huge herds of antelope in the distance. Two or three thousand animals ran in front of us at the edge of the swamp and jumped over some obstruction in their path, the herd appearing to be a huge rising and falling wave. A magnificent horde of about thirty-five hundred Thomson's gazelle were a feast for the eyes. Then, before we could settle down on our path once again, another enormous herd of probably two thousand zebra came thundering through, about five hundred yards from where we lay hidden among the mopani trees. The profusion of animals was absolutely astounding. Not only were the varieties mind-boggling, but also the size of the herds was unbelievable. On our walks, over a couple of days, we saw elephant, waterbuck, lechwe, sebogarta (or reedbuck), green parrots, black-faced monkeys, duikers, giraffe, eland, gemsbok, a pride of lions, a cheetah, a giraffe, and a caracal. There were brown and spotted hyenas, aardwolves, civets, zorillas (black-and-white polecats), cane rats, mongooses, and honey ratels.

We also saw herds of buffalo, sitatunga, zebra, impala, and tsessebe. We sat in the shelter of a tree, a large *Ficus ingens,* locally known as a moomu tree. We saw herd after herd run towards the water. There, they would mingle and relax before returning at a measured pace. Then, just as suddenly, something would spook them and they would gather and gallop off at great speed and in a very excitable mood. When this happened, we suspected the presence of some marauder. What a delight to see herds in these vast numbers. Each herd was different, but most numbered in the thousands.

We walked on, in this enchanted land, wondering what new marvel would present itself. All of a sudden, I disappeared and found myself up to my shoulders in a large hole in the ground. I gave a shriek of fright, and my companions came over to see what had befallen me. I was laughing so hard at my misadventure when, lo and behold, four small baby warthogs climbed over me in great haste and enthusiasm, squeaking with cries of fright, and disappeared into the bush. I was extricated from the warthog abode with difficulty. I thought the matter was funny, I was weak with laughter. The story of my mishap made it back to camp that night. Over dinner, I was teased unmercifully about my ridiculous fall down the warthog den.

Bobby was very friendly with Kweri. Because of this, we, as a group, were privileged to stay in one of the camps used by the River Bushmen who were sixty or so in number. These people did not wear clothes in our sense of the word. The women draped an animal skin around their waists, perhaps added a smaller skin around their necks, donned some animal bones or beads, and were dressed for the day. Young and old were bare-breasted. Many a young mother placed a child on her hip, plunged a nipple into the child's mouth, and continued with her chores. The River Bushmen are non-Bantu Africans. Their features are quite different from those of the other local tribes. For one thing, their features, non-Negroid, are very much smaller in size. They have very high cheekbones, slender high foreheads, and elegantly slender noses. They reminded me of images on early Egyptian tombs. They did not live in traditional huts but under the trees, and their beds were made of a few sticks with skins draped over the top. They appeared also to sleep on skins. I saw a few small children asleep in these little places in the shade and on the soft skins of the wild herds. The particular tribes along the Kwaai were thought to have been remnants of Semitic tribes originally from the region of the Nile in North Africa. The department of anthropology of the University of the Witwatersrand conducted studies on the origins of the River Bushmen, and this was their tentative conclusion.

We camped in the River Bushmen's "village." When we arrived, we did not see many men. I was feeling very dry, dusty, and dirty after our forays into the plains to see the herds, so I took myself off to the river for a wash. I decided that the only way I might accomplish this was to stand on the front end of a beached canoe. This way, I could bend towards the waterline with washcloth in hand and attempt to wash whatever parts of my body were available. I had to be a contortionist. On the shore, I noticed that a group of young female River Bushmen had gathered.

They were hysterical at my antics, but also curious at my attempt to wash my grimy face in crocodile-infested waters. I finished my ministrations by dabbing some 4711 lavender water on my neck under my long hair. They came up to me as I left the mokoro (dugout canoe) and sniffed me. They pulled at their faces, indicating that they thought I had a horrible scent! Of course, I knew that people's reactions to odours were culturally conditioned, so I returned the compliment, indicating that they, who, in fact, never, ever bathed, had an equally awful scent!

Washing removes dirt and oils from the skin, obviously, but the Bushmen thought that leaving their skin encrusted provided a measure of protection from insect bites. I found it interesting that the men all carried with them a "swishing" cane, a short cane usually with the end part of a warthog's tail tied to it with tree fibres. These they constantly swished as they went about their business. It prevented the tsetse flies, and others carrying cerebral malaria, from landing on their skin and transmitting deadly diseases.

On our last evening with the River Bushmen, people gathered to say farewell. There were about eighty people present. The ranks of the locals swelled, and I was surprised to find different groups of people from Namibia among them. These people were very different in looks. They tended to be extremely tall; most of the men were over six feet in height. As they danced in a circle, they dwarfed the River Bushmen. The Namibian women did not participate in the dance but remained seated beneath a tree off to the side. After being accustomed to the nudity of the River Bushmen, they were a real shock to the eyes.

These Namibians belonged to the Herero tribe just across the border and had been the object of a concerted "attack" by the early missionaries, who disapproved of their nudity and persuaded them to dress themselves to imitate Victorian women. They now wore long dresses in riotous colours, embellished with leg-of-mutton sleeves. On their heads were wrapped headdresses, some about a foot in height. As the women tended to be tall in the first place, they now towered above me by at least a foot and a half. I noticed that they were stately and had beautiful faces that were full of smiles when they approached us. It seems that a similar thing had happened in Hawaii when missionaries arrived. They were horrified at the indigenous people's laissez-faire attitude to life and their display of nude breasts, so they rapidly persuaded the local women to enshroud their bodies in muumuus!

The Herero women did not fit easily into this primitive environment and, to me, were an anachronism. They seemed to get on well with the River Bushmen, but I think that they secretly thought them to be more primitive.

One afternoon, Bobby took Tom and me in his truck via a convoluted route to a small clearing in the bush on an island on the banks of the Thamalakane. It was here that I was fortunate to meet June Kaye. June was a very attractive petite woman with piercing eyes, short dark brown hair, a determined expression, and a riveting personality. Her home was comprised of several rondavels (round mud houses) with thatched roofs, separated from one another by twenty or thirty feet of hard earth.

After the obligatory introductions, we were offered seats in the open, under a large tree, where tea was served.

June earned a living by writing. She had just published the book *Okavango,* which was met with some acclaim. She had an "office" where she wrote every day, and she had given orders that while she was there hammering away at an old typewriter, she was not to be disturbed.

Close by was a larger hut, the door of which was covered over with netting. I presumed this to be her bedroom. Several other huts obviously served other functions. The open area in which we sat was covered in thatch but was otherwise open to the elements. Bobby had had a long-standing relationship with June and her husband. They had gone croc hunting together and all had an intense love of this gloriously lush land.

June was married young and had three children. Her daughter had no liking for the wild and so, when June came to the Okavango to live permanently, she was left in Bulawayo with her grandmother to attend school. June's two little boys, who were not yet of school age, had come along to Botswana with their parents.

June married when she was very young, when her husband had been demobbed after the Second World War. The couple had built a home in the Matopos Hills of Southern Rhodesia (now Zimbabwe).

June had always been crazy about animals. She and her husband had built a farm, and June had always had a menagerie of wild animals. She would have liked to have worked with animals, but this was impossible as long as she lived within the city limits. Having been educated in South Africa, she had always wanted to be a zoologist. Both she and her husband had decided that city living was not to their liking and that wild places and bush living appealed to them. June had been very close to her father, but after he died of a sudden heart attack, she felt that there was no longer a reason to stay in Zimbabwe.

Southern Rhodesia (now Zimbabwe) had been in the political limelight and was going through a difficult transition period, and this provided the Kayes with more impetus to leave their homeland.

So, having sold off all their tangible assets, the family moved to the Bechuanaland Protectorate, now Botswana.

Robert had been the first to come up with the idea. At first, it seemed preposterous, but with the difficult period in Rhodesia (Zimbabwe.), June was persuaded to try out the idea to live and explore the magnificent array of animal life in Botswana.

She brought her two small sons with her. Later, she decided to send the older boy home to her mother when he attained school age. Oliver, her youngest boy, had only just very recently attained the age where he would be flown back to stay with his grandmother and attend school.

We had a pleasant introduction and a conversation over tea and biscuits, during which I had found out the details of June's life. She suddenly excused herself and disappeared behind the "kitchen" hut. She reappeared, then asked us to follow her.

Sitting in the shade behind one of the mopani trees was a huge male lion. He was spread out, asleep, perfectly at home, and paying no attention to the new visitors. Tom was immediately entranced. He had always gone about burdened with an array of cameras and photographic equipment, and his eyes twinkled at the possibilities the lion presented to his photographic eye. June had brought with her a large bottle of castor oil and an enormous ladle, and proceeded to make the recalcitrant lion open his mouth and swallow the spoonful. She explained that the Lion was always constipated as June was not always able to feed him fresh kill. Tom's photos of the lion were displayed in a photographic exhibition years later, in the main library in Vancouver to much acclaim, when Tom returned to Canada.

June and her husband negotiated the swamps aboard an amphibious vehicle, which had been war surplus and which they had bought in England. This solved the problem of safety, as well as a great way to negotiate the difficult canals full of peril. It was their home in the Okavango waters.

*   *   *

I was born in Africa by accident. I lived in South Africa for thirty-five years of my life. South Africa made indelible marks on my psyche. Some days, living in Canada, my mind plays tricks on me. I look at the seagulls flying overhead and imagine that I see vultures circling instead. I have often awakened in the night and mistaken the sounds of the night for the cries of baboons in the trees. I also hear the phantom beating of distant drums in the hours of the dawn. I hallucinate about the roar of a lion in the dark, when in fact I am in Canada, so far from any Lion's roar. It is merely the roar of a passing vehicle…

A part of me will always be homesick for the wide open spaces, the visions of the herds galloping across the savannahs, a million pink flamingos darkening the sky in the pans, the bright brassy light of the sun on the yellow waving grasses, and the basso profundo of an African man singing as he wends his way home in the night. I always recall the most incredible adventure of my life – the time I spent getting to know the vast swamps of the Okavango. Few people have had the privilege of getting to know the amazing cultures of the River Bushmen, the San, and the Herero in their natural habitats; of living in a village of River Bushmen; of fishing in the backwaters of the swamp for bream; or of going crocodile hunting with one of the truly great crocodile hunters of his time.

Bobby Wilmot's organizing our days enabled all of us on the safari to experience things that others only dream about. I often wondered what happened to Bobby since I moved to Canada. I recently found out that he had met a dreadfully painful end in the backwaters of the swamps he loved, where he was still hunting for his crocodiles. He was bitten by a black mamba snake while on a foray into a distant area of the swamp. He had, at the time, only two of the four anti-venum injections that were needed to save his life. He died on his boat in the middle of the night, with only his croc-hunting companions at his side. It was a very painful death. I am sure that all who knew him mourned his loss. I will always remember him fondly.

During our stay at his camp on the Thamalakane, he ventured out on so many nights to hunt crocodile. It is estimated that he was responsible for single-handedly wiping out twenty thousand crocs in his forays over twenty years. Today, the number of crocodiles is severely limited. The crocs hide out in the backwaters of the swamps, where it is illegal to shoot them.

Gone now, too, are the masses of hunters armed to the teeth and bent on slaughter. The history had been one of blood and guts, greed and gore. From the time of Livingstone, the area had been attacked by waves of human predators. By 1867, over twelve thousand elephants had been killed, their tusks swapped for beads. Soon after, the African tribes were introduced to rifles and undertook a slaughter of all the rhino in short order. Then the buffalo, their numbers depleted, fled northwards from the predations of the hunters. Today, only less than two thousand elephants remain.

June Kaye and her husband were responsible for initiating the idea of forming what was to become the Moremi Game Reserve. They had had to persuade the governing bodies as well as the local tribes that it was in their best interest to preserve their incredible heritage. There was much procrastination and even dissent, but on the final vote, the tribes came together with rare insight and voted to establish a game reserve in the Okavango to protect the extraordinary animals and amazing peoples in their midst. Kaye recalls these times in her book *The Thirteenth Moon,* which makes for amazing reading.

I had also wondered what fate had befallen the extraordinary June Kaye, whom I had encountered in her camp on the island on the Thamalakane, with her family and her pet lion, and cruising in the backwaters of the swamp in her amphibious vehicle.

She wrote two more books detailing her extraordinary life. She remarried and has moved to Europe with her new husband.

I shall never, for the rest of my life, ever forget that I was, in fact, one of the few outsiders who had the chance to live in the territory in its early days, when it was, indeed, like living West of the sun and East of the moon.

MY FAMILY HISTORY

My maternal grandmother, Carolina, was an extraordinary woman. When I was a child, she was the light of my life. All my memories of a contented childhood revolve around her.

As an only child who lacked playmates, did not speak English, and was of a different culture, I was quite isolated, but my grandmother made up for this by inventing games, telling stories, and weaving her magic to keep me occupied and happy for hours. When I awakened early to a sleeping household, I crept into her bed for a cuddle and sunk deeply into her welcoming arms. She and I would play the gancho game, which consisted of hiding a large hairpin from my grandmother's hair somewhere in the folds of the bed. While I attempted to find it, there would be much tickling and giggling, all in hushed tones so as not to wake the sleeping household. The gancho would eventually appear in all sorts of magical places (once behind Gran's ear). When I finally found it, I would shriek with delight and be assured of how clever I was in uncovering it in such a tricky place!

I always knew that I was loved unconditionally. Gran's open heart extended to my son Robyn from the time he was a tiny baby. She adored him and spent as much time with him as she had done with me, giving him her undivided attention and love.

The Portuguese equivalent of *great-grandmother* is *bisavo.* Over time, it became *bicha,* and the diminutive *bichinha* was my grandmother's nickname till the day she died. The nearest translation of *bichinha* is "little tiny creature." My grandmother left a legacy of nothing material but did leave behind the greatest gift one could ever bestow, that of unconditional love. She had loved, and been loved intensely by, three generations.

I recall that she adored the garden and tended the fruit trees, fighting off any approaching birds that had seen our ripened fruit. Her ferocity knew no bounds. She collected small paper bags and put them over each fig as it ripened, and then mocked the birds she had thwarted. Finally, when the fruit was ready to eat, she redeemed it and brought the figs into the kitchen as offerings to her favourites. The children always got the best, but Gran would sometimes relent and hold back a particularly tasty morsel for my father, later giving it to him in an offhanded manner!

Despite her smiling face and loving manner, she had led a sad and deprived life. The second youngest of six siblings, all girls, she had been placed, at the age of five, in a girls' convent school in Lisbon. Her father, a philanderer, had married her mother at a very young age, mainly for the

Cork estates that she had inherited in the south of Portugal. He then proceeded to sell them off to pay gambling debts and the bills incurred by his riotous living. The family came into hard times. My great-grandmother was neglected and fell into a deep depression. She no longer took interest in the home, withdrew from any and all household chores, and retired to her room with the blinds pulled and the room darkened amid the bright Lisbon sunshine.

Her condition did not improve; in fact, it seemed to have deteriorated. The children no longer came home at weekends but remained in the gloomy surroundings of the cloister, looked after by nuns. Home visits were sporadic at best. Over time, the children's mother ceased to interact with them altogether. Their father continued to have the proverbial good time, and the girls visited only occasionally to have an isolated existence in a darkened house. I understand that had they not all been together in the same place growing up, they would have experienced almost no normal family interaction. They did, however, seem to mother one another, and they were a tightly knit group. Carolina, my grandmother, was mothered by two older sisters who must have done a magnificent job, because she grew up with a fine sensibility of loving and giving and was of a stable and happy disposition.

When my Great-Aunts were of the age to return home, they went in a group of three, at first, and thereafter married quickly. Carolina, being one of the youngest, went home with the last three girls, the youngest being only thirteen. I suspect that my gran was, at that time, an innocent creature, not able to assess the men around her or their evil intentions. She had had little experience of the world and knew not the realities of living in a Victorian society. She was pure of heart, and so it was almost inevitable, what with her having a difficult social standing, a demented mother, and an uncaring father, that she should have fallen desperately in love with my grandfather, a dashing and debonair aristocrat from a rich and prestigious family who promised her the world, attention, and undying love. I do not know how they met, because the matter was never discussed. She lived her later life as if he had never existed. It was only when I was an adult that I pieced things together from the remarks made by family members.

Carolina, who had two children with my grandfather, never married but was, by all accounts, ecstatically happy. She was totally undemanding and thought that my grandfather loved her as much as she loved him. Unfortunately, he had no intention of marrying beneath his class. In any case he was infatuated with a Parisian courtesan, a woman of great beauty and panache, with whom he also had a child, almost at the same time as Carolina. My half-Aunt, Marie Antoinette was a little younger than my mother, so it seems to me that my grandfather was stringing along both women – and who knows how many more – with his charm, wit, money, and good looks.

My grandfather also got into a good deal of trouble with the authorities. I understand that he was the quintessential snob. He was mortified that Portugal had done away with the monarchy and become a republic in 1910. He was involved in a treasonous plot to overthrow the government and was betrayed. Because of his social standing, it was intimated that, in order to avoid being charged with treason, he had no choice but to leave the country, post-haste.

In those days, the wealthy immigrated to Brazil. My grandfather went, with stealth and little notice, off to Rio, leaving both his families behind and in the lurch. He did, however, decide that his daughter Lydia, my mother's sister, would be useful in Rio to look after him. At the age of fourteen, Lydia went off precipitously, to Brazil. Bicha was separated from her oldest child, never to see her again.

Women during that period did not work; gentlewomen, at least, did not go outside the home to make money. My grandmother was left broken-hearted and totally destitute, with no family money or resources and no husband – and an indifferent father and a young daughter to support.

I have no idea how she coped, but I do know that this episode marked her for life. She never looked at another man. As before, she retreated to the only family she had known: her sisters. She rallied and tried to bring up my mother as best she could in a small back room in the house of Adelaide, her older sister. But I do know that her experiences had changed her drastically. It was as if she had reorganized her priorities, come out of her trance, and decided that she was going to do whatever she had to do to give my mother the best life she could in such desperate circumstances.

Adelaide herself was not rich, but she had married a gentle man who not only loved her but also gave her whatever she wanted. He (who sports a handlebar moustache in the photo I have of him) was a lawyer by profession, but his real passion was dogs. He had a household full of terriers. Because he and his wife had not had children, they treated the dogs as family. The dogs' food was specially prepared every day by the maid, and the dogs were combed, brushed, cuddled, and endlessly loved. Unfortunately, Adelaide's husband was also crazy about chocolates and indulged his passion. There were always fine Parisian chocolates in the house. In view of his love affair with his animals, he thought it only fair to give them these precious titbits, liberally. It was not generally understood that dogs were not able to eat cocoa products and that, in fact, these are quite poisonous to poor little terriers. The dogs seemed to die with great regularity, sometimes even as very young dogs. My great-uncle was mystified and mortified and could not understand how dogs so well treated and loved should die with such monotonous regularity.

When my mother went to live with Adelaide, the other sister, who was named Julia, also lived with them. Julia was tiny, under five feet in height, and had never married. She had an indomitable spirit and was a mover and a shaker. Adelaide was quite different; she was placid, appeared slightly plump, and had a generous and self-effacing nature. She was also quite beautiful.

Mom was certainly loved by her aunts, but she had few things as a child. She was only able to complete elementary school, which, in Lisbon, was called grade four. It provided her with a basic education, but, as a highly intelligent little girl, she felt the loss of her home and her father very deeply and developed an inability to continue her studies. She longed to play the piano, but, of course, there was no money for lessons.

Mom had made friends with a rich girl named Olga. Olga was plump, indolent, and unattractive, but she had the key to further learning. Olga had a tutor who gave her French lessons daily. My mother would go over every day to play with her friend, but she insisted that Olga do her homework first. Out came the French lesson books, and my mother "helped" Olga do her daily assignments. It was only when they were adults that Olga realized that there was a method to the madness. My mother got her education second-hand, so to speak. Her uncle taught her numbers and provided her with books of classical literature and poetry to read. She read avidly, but aspired to so much more. My Mother, who retired to Lisbon when my father died in South Africa, remained a close friend of Olga Catarino. I visited Aunt Olga recently on my last trip to Europe. I keep in touch with her son, who has always been one of my closest friends.

While living in Adelaide's house, Bicha scrounged old clothes and hand-me-downs from everyone in her family and Olga's family. Bicha was an innovative seamstress and had quite a sense of style. She once cut down an overcoat belonging to Olga's father and made a delicious little winter coat for my mother, all lined in the silk from a cast-off dress. Everyone remarked how fabulous it was. At Olga's house, everyone patted and admired it but did not recognize its origin. Mom, not disabusing them of the notion that it was a most expensive winter garment, let them believe that she had purchased it from an upscale boutique.

It seemed as if all the women of the time were taught to knit, crochet, embroider, and tat. My grandmother did all four, and her sewing was a thing of beauty to behold. As she had no sewing machine, all her handiwork was done in minuscule stitches by the light of a kerosene lamp. I have kept some examples of her handiwork, as she liked to make me dresses when I was a child. I cannot believe, even today, her meticulous work.

While Lydia and my mom, Deolinda, lived at home, they went out dressed beautifully and showed impeccable taste, but they always wore dresses made from this and that. It is interesting to note that despite my gran's accomplishments, these items were not remarked upon as things of value. I always think that, were she alive today, Bicha would be regaled as a marvellous designer.

When Lydia departed for Rio, she went with the understanding that she would have a better life and, with her father's social standing, a plethora of opportunities to marry far better than if she remained in Lisbon as the illegitimate daughter of a mother of few means. For these reasons, Bicha let her go with goodwill but also with a heavy heart.

So, Lydia bid her mother and sister adieu and set sail for Brazil with her dashing father. She was blonde and green-eyed (like her father) and quite a beauty, with long slender legs, a vivacity for life, and a love of extravagances. When she settled in Rio, she took up sailing, rode a horse reasonably well, ordered her clothes from Paris, bred borzoi dogs, and generally hobnobbed with people of high society. She took lessons in French and presented herself as a dashing lady about town. Her father indulged her. After so many years of seeing him only sporadically, she was beginning to enjoy the high life to which she had felt entitled.

In her chauffeur-driven car, she wrote long letters to her mother in which she detailed her life, including pictures of herself dressed in wispy chiffon creations, displaying gorgeous legs, dimpled knees, and high-heel Parisian shoes in the trendiest style. And always, there were the two borzoi dogs. Lydia learnt to fence and paint. In fact, when my mother died, there were several of Lydia's oil paintings in the Lisbon apartment. In those early years, my Mother looked at the photographs of Lydia, read the letters, and said nothing.

After my mother's death in Lisbon in her mid-eighties, I went through her papers and found all the pictures Lydia had sent home during that period. They were in a cigar box tied with pink ribbons. They numbered at least a hundred.

The temperament of the two sisters was chalk and cheese. My mother developed a sense of determination to succeed. She was dead serious about life.

Lydia married a dashing cavalry officer and continued her socialite lifestyle, concentrating on having a good time. She later divorced her husband. The entire family was in a state of shock because, to them, regardless of the hand one might be dealt in life, divorce was just too terrible a deed to contemplate, let alone indulge in. In Lisbon, such a barbaric act was not even legally possible. For many years under Portuguese law called the Concordata, an agreement was made between Portugal and the Vatican to outlaw civil divorce altogether! Divorce was not only not allowed, but also was not even available in the civil courts. I recall as a teenager meeting people who had fled Portugal and gone to other, more liberal countries with their lovers, and sometimes with children from their union, because there was never any hope of creating a legitimate family at home. The Catholic Church was at its most repressive in Portugal throughout the centuries and continued to demand a pound of flesh from its beleaguered citizens well into the late twentieth century.

In any case, my mother grew up with strong feelings of abandonment and rejection. She dreamed of becoming respectable, climbing the social ladder, and being accepted. She was a pretty little thing under five feet in height, with enormous green eyes and long eyelashes. Her hair was blonde and quite curly. She, too, had the straight, slim legs with the dimpled knees. Where Lydia had always been fun-loving, Deolinda was shy and serious. Where Lydia was a free spirit, my mother was strait-laced, her dominant characteristic always one of conformity. My mother never questioned, and always obeyed, the dictates of society, no matter how unreasonable, in her effort to be accepted. Lydia did not care what society thought. She set trends, showed off her talents, and laughed at the ridiculousness of the protocols and the straitjackets imposed by the middle class.

Once, when she arrived back in Lisbon to visit the family, she caused quite a furore. She was happy, gay, and obviously having a great time. That she had returned a divorced woman, having so recently disposed of her husband yet remaining in a hilarious mood, was unconscionable! Lydia went off to Paris and then returned to kiss the family goodbye, going back to Rio in a cloud of French perfume, remarking that she longed to see her beloved dogs and could not wait a moment longer to kiss and hug them.

She had acquired a Brazilian accent and used all the Brazilian colloquialisms, which the Lisbon people giggled, considering them very provincial. The Brazilians have "babified" the Portuguese tongue. For example, the word *diferente* (meaning "different") is pronounced "diferen-chee." In the Brazilian version, the most unlikely words are made into diminutives. A large man may show affection by using the diminutive (not available in English), which, in translation, is equivalent to, "Little lady, give me a little bottle with little aspirins." To the people in Lisbon, this was merely ridiculous, but they humoured those who came to visit as errant relatives who were guilty of the massacre of the mellifluous language that is Portuguese.

Seeking conformity for the Portuguese language in modern times was no mean feat. A commission was established to guarantee the "purity of the language," but I think that the only successes have been in the areas of adapting appropriate words to encompass new technology. The sprawling lands of Brazil have produced magnificent new writers who have revealed and reflected on the Brazilian experience. While in Rio, I bought an *Aurélio Dictionary of the Portuguese Language,* which is Brazilian Portuguese's equivalent to the *Oxford English Dictionary.* So many words in the Aurélio dictionary reflect the nature of Brazilian culture. In a regular Lisbon Portuguese dictionary, under a list of names of the fruits from the Amazon region, acai is certainly not to be found!

Lydia returned home and continued her high life as before, not knowing that she was soon to be marred in a terrible accident. Lydia prided herself on playing the piano well, and she played Chopin with verve and vigour. She also liked to shop. Once, while ascending an elevator in an elegant store in downtown Rio, she became irritated with the elevator that, for some reason, would not start. In order to determine whether the outer metal folding grid door was secured, she slipped her hand through the inner grid gate. Suddenly, the elevator lurched into a start before Lydia could extricate herself. Worse, she caught her hand in the door. When her rings got entangled in the metal of the grid work, she was lifted bodily as the elevator descended, screaming her way through two levels while her fingers were almost torn from their sockets and large chunks of flesh torn from the bone. She passed out and was rushed to hospital, in shock. She had many surgeries, but her fingers were permanently damaged. She was never again able to play her beloved piano.

Although Bicha had not had seen her daughter since that wrenching day when she left at the age of fourteen, she was utterly devastated when she heard the news, many months later, after Lydia was more or less recovered. My father initially refused to tell Bicha the bad news and waited until all the operations were completed. Then, he took her aside and told her all the details. Bicha cried for days, said nothing, and went about for a week with eyes swollen with grief.

Lydia eventually married an American and went to live in Lake Tahoe. She does not appear to be quite as well off as she had been previously. Pictures of her sitting in the kitchen of a modest apartment tell a story of her having come down in life. Her second husband died, and almost immediately afterwards, she found that she had breast cancer. She had no medical insurance so found herself in dire circumstances. At this point, she wrote to my mother and asked for five hundred dollars so that she might get chemotherapy.

The letter was read at the table at dinner. Bicha was terrified for her daughter and wept. My mother refused to send Lydia the money. After all, she said, Lydia had spent her entire life having a good time, so why had she not looked towards her declining years and saved some of her money? My Mother had worked all her life, had never indulged in extravagances, and had always been most cautious about money. Why, indeed, should she send Lydia anything?

Bicha was mortified but said nothing. She could not remedy the situation herself, as she had no money of her own, apart from some that my father slipped to her occasionally. The argument raged. My father then took control of the situation and said that, regardless, he would wire the money to Lydia. At this point, my mother insisted on a caveat. Should anything happen to Lydia, then her rings and jewels were to be deeded to my mother. She insisted with such determination that my father finally capitulated. That her sister was in terrible straits was of no great concern to my mother. I could sense my mother's jealousy and rage at the good fortune of her sister over the years, and her own sense of abandonment and loss. That her only sister was dying did not quite enter into her consciousness or her calculations. I saw the sense of injustice that gripped my mother's mind and the motivations that had propelled her forward towards achieving her goals. I pitied her at that moment. The curtain had been momentarily lifted, and I had glimpsed a corner of her soul; I never looked at her quite the same again, and I never forgot that conversation at the dinner table so many aeons ago.

We heard no more from Lydia, She died alone, a pauper in an American hospital, with no family to bid her farewell. My Mother was quite enraged when she did not receive the jewels she had been promised. They had been sold to pay for the kennels and the upkeep of Lydia's three dogs. It seemed to me that, right to the end, Lydia never got her priorities right.

*　　*　　*

The Portuguese ethic had always favoured men. Women were to be seen, displayed, and then kept home – and definitely not heard. There was, and still is, a cult of "mom-ism." Boys in the family have intense relationships with their mothers and are spoiled and babied right into adulthood. It was customary for boys to stay in the family home until such a time as they were established and at an age to marry. Only then did they leave. Women had few independent rights, and laws did not protect females – they protected families. Errant females were generally ostracized, not only by relatives but also by the other females in the society, as they posed a threat to the conformity of women within the family. Men generally did whatever they chose, and society turned a blind eye. Until very recently, women needed only one thing to be accepted and cherished, and that was virginity.

One cannot underestimate the long-term effects of the Moorish occupation of the Iberian Peninsula. Certainly, the repression of women was codified during that period and so entrenched during this epoch that when Portugal finally cast off the Moorish yoke, the Catholic Church stepped into the breach and took over where the Moors had left off. The idea of women's being cloistered, hidden away, and restricted to working in their homes – and severely deprived of civil rights – was sanctioned from this period onwards. Women automatically lost the rights to their children if they moved out of the family home. Draconian laws were put in place in the name of "maintaining the family." The Church did not curtail itself to the promulgation of religious laws but wielded so much power over matters that in other countries were considered civil matters. The lines between State Law and Cannon Law were totally obscured. Portugal always had great difficulty in separating Church and State. It was only in the late twentieth century when things began to improve. The status of women remained almost mediaeval long after the rest of Europe had moved to cast off those oppressive ideas. The cynical pretence was kept up, the implication being that these laws were for the protection of women in general and of the family in particular. The women were the sacrificial lambs at the altar, by which the family was maintained. But the reality was that the subjugation of women, and the social fabric, was most unforgiving. There were only two kinds of women, "good" and "bad," and the difference was predicated on the extent of a woman's sexual activity. There was a glaring double standard.

This, then, was the scenario into which my Mother had been cast. Despite being brought up in a convent, my grandmother was not religious. She tolerated the church but took it with large pinches of salt, giggling at the absurdity of it all. Living, as she later did, in South Africa, she could afford to feel free and untethered for the first time in her life.

My mother, on the other hand, took the idea of being virtuous and blame-free as the only capital which she could expend.

My mother and father married and remained devoted to each other till the day death separated them, and beyond. My father adored my mother. A year after they moved to Johannesburg, I arrived on the scene. As soon as my Mother knew that she was expecting a baby, she sent for my grandmother, who was there from the moment when I appeared screaming injury to the world, when the doctor pulled me out with metal instruments. I still carry the scars that were left by this rough initiation!

The new land and the fresh ideas did not alter the ingrained thinking of my parents, who continued to view the world through European eyes and the constraints of semi-mediaeval thinking. They knew who they were; they understood their values and made attempt to indoctrinate their growing daughter. I, however, had other examples of life around me on which to model my existence, and I resisted most of their teaching in matters of values and ideology. I embarrassed the priest by asking, in relation to Adam and Eve, what language they had spoken? At the age of nine,

I knew in a flash of sudden illumination that all the catechism I was being taught was, as I wrote in my diary, a "bunch of twaddle." I was a rebel at an early age!

I think one needs to be careful about introducing young children to adults with distinctly subversive ideas. In my case, my father had a wonderfully talented cellist friend called San Vicent, who played weekly with him on Sunday mornings in a Haydn string quartet. San Vicent sounded like Pablo Casals and spent his days either playing or arranging classical music. He was a madrileño who continued to speak poor English but was tremendously knowledgeable about music. My father loved to play with him. His happiest moments were when the two of them retired to the back of the house to make music.

San Vicent had a wife who was a London Jewess. She was tall and elegant, had attended the best universities, and stood in great contrast to her husband, who was short, fat, and terribly interested in gourmet food. Mrs San Vicent was the kind of person who was content with burnt toast and could not boil water. A more incongruous couple could not be found anywhere. But they adored each other with a passion, and the marriage endured while more likely matches failed. Mrs San Vicent was a true intellectual. Her name was Ethel. Once my father asked her to tutor me, at age nine, in English and reading, she was like a breath of fresh air in my staid surroundings. She had a twinkle in her eye and liked to hold contrary opinions. She had majored in philosophy at Oxford, in the days when few women attempted such feats, and seemed to possess encyclopaedic knowledge. She had two sons, both of whom were Oxford dons.

Auntie Ethel, as I called her, was, as I said, the breath of fresh air in the staid and conformist home in which I had grown up. She always asked why questions and encouraged me to do the same. She not only helped my reading and vocabulary improve but also rattled both my mind and soul. I learnt the most astounding things from her and thought that this rather plain and ungainly woman was magical. I sensed that I should not discuss her ideas with my unsuspecting parents. I grew to dearly love the woman who made my mind and my spirit take wing.

To come to the realization that nothing was at it seemed, that so-called constants should be queried, that no human being had the final answers to the mysteries of existence, that one interpretation was probably as good as another, and that the great poets and playwrights probably gave us more glimpses of reality than anyone else, was heady stuff. Aunt Ethel had marked me for life. What a contrast to the boredom of life in a convent school, with uninspiring and indoctrinating teachers who were ready to proclaim even the most innocuous thing sinful. After my experience with Auntie Ethel, their ideas were mundane and even repulsive. I looked at the nuns as women who had floundered along the way and were attempting to perpetuate myths. I hated the Bible stories. I thought them cruel and arbitrary, and they only served to alienate me further. I sat stonily in classes of Christian apologetics, awoke each morning to go to Mass with a book of English verse rather than a prayer book, and allowed religion to flow all around me but leave me relatively unscathed. Auntie Ethel would have much to answer for!

LEAVING PORTUGAL

My parents had, through the vagaries of fate, left Portugal almost as soon as they were married and then immigrated to South Africa from Portugal. They had never had the opportunity to travel and were both excited to go to new pastures. On both sides of the family, there seemed to be generations of Portuguese all clinging to the ancestral lands. They pitied those less fortunate who, through accidents of fate, had gone to other territories under Portuguese jurisdiction but not necessarily of the same culture.

For generations, everyone was solidly attached to the umbilical cord of the Motherland. Some rose to prominence, but the umbilical cord remained firmly attached.

My maternal grandmother, who was a remarkable woman, had been brought up in difficult circumstances and continued to wind herself into an even more difficult life. I have been told that her father had lands in the south that were productive and produced cork, but that he was a man who lived the good life without regard to his means. He ended up with five daughters, plus a wife who was always depressed. In her final days, she retreated into her house and never left. The five girls grew up in a convent and received a very poor education, but they remained together and helped each other along, the oldest looking after the life of the youngest. They never went home and got to the stage where they had hardly any recollection of their mother. Things became worse when the cork properties were sold. In despair, their father became an alcoholic.

The oldest of my maternal Aunts was fortunate enough to marry a lawyer. He was a jolly, well-disposed, and rather rotund man who was of a loving disposition and fiercely attached to his dogs. He was also a sucker for a sob story. One by one, he brought his wife's beleaguered sisters to stay with him so that they could live in good surroundings and find suitable husbands of the same class. He was always in an expansive mood and wanted the best for everyone. But, above all, he was entranced by anything on four legs. He bought cigars for himself but never forgot to buy flowing boxes of chocolates for his dogs. They repaid his largesse by promptly getting ill and dying from mysterious ailments, which at the time had not been diagnosed. Had he lived today, he would have realized that the dogs were poisoned by his kindness in sharing the ubiquitous chocolates, which, to dogs, are deadly.

One by one, my Great-Aunts came to live in Lisbon and all married well. Unfortunately, my grandmother did not share the same fate. She was quite attractive with piercing blue eyes and a jolly disposition. She met a man, quite by accident, who had been titled, and was led sadly astray. Despite family objections, she went to live with him. In time, she had two daughters, my aunt Lydia and my mother, Deolinda.

Portugal was then going through a phase where the monarchy was permanently discarded and the country became a republic. The king was exiled to Brazil. Things went on without any violence or revolution. The problem was that those who had considered themselves aristocrats were not pleased with the turn of affairs, were plotting against the government, and were not leaving well enough alone. My grandfather was one of the discontented who was plotting a revolution. My grandmother was very unhappy with the turn of events, but she only realized the seriousness of the plots that were being hatched when three police arrived on her doorstep and informed my grandfather that he had been implicated in a plot against the government. They told him that he must choose between going to jail immediately and being accused of treason or leaving the country right away – and permanently.

A decision had to be made within twenty-four hours! My grandfather opted to leave the country. On the spur of the moment, he decided that he would not go alone and that my aunt Lydia, his older daughter, would come with him. My mother was too young to be of any assistance to him and, in fact, would probably be a burden, so he bid the family farewell, bought a passage to Brazil, and left the next day, without making any arrangements to support the family he left behind. So it was that my grandmother was left in Lisbon with my mother, then a small girl only nine years old. The two moved in with my grandmother's sister in Lisbon, in the house bursting with a menagerie of dogs.

My grandmother, very artistic, was able to make clothes from discarded garments donated by the family. She made heart-stopping couture-style winter coats styled from hand-me-downs. My mother, despite not having anything to her name, was always well dressed and, in fact, often better-dressed than her school companions, due, in large part, to the loving ministrations of her mother.

In those days, compulsory education ended at grade-four level, and so my Mother, who was quite bright and studious, was forced to leave school, with no hope of continuing her education. She nevertheless found ingenious ways to further her education. She became friendly with a girl named Olga. They would spend time together, during which my mother "helped" Olga with her homework each afternoon. In the process, she picked up French as well as history and math.

My Mother was very musical. In order to practice "piano" without a piano per se, she tore an old sheet to strips, attached it to an old table, and drew the keyboard on it. When she was finished "practicing," she carefully rolled up her "piano" until her next foray into learning music. She led a very sheltered life with little or no exposure to Lisbon society, but she soldiered on valiantly. Her Father continued to pretend that she did not exist. The only love she got was from her dog-loving uncle, who loved everyone anyway.

My Mother's sister Lydia, on the other hand, landed on her feet. She was accepted into society in Rio because of her father's connections and had a privileged life. There were country club affiliations, borzoi dogs, and stables of horses to ride. She sent home pictures of herself at soirées with minor royalty and during outings on thoroughbred horses in the company of magnificent military men, dressed de rigueur. All this while, my poor Mother was almost homeless. If she had a roof over her head, it was because of the kindness of strangers.

Fate took a hand when my Mother was asked to go with a girlfriend to a music festival on one of the local beaches. She dressed carefully and wore an apron on which were embroidered and appliquéd representations of fruit. She was helping out a friend at one of the fruit stalls.

She could have had no idea whatsoever that her future life would be decided on that weekend. My father, a violinist who had graduated from the conservatory of music, had offered to help out and provide music at the festival. On the surface of things, it was an improbable meeting.

My father had seen my mother and went around to several friends, trying to get an introduction. He was rather shy but, in any case, wanted to be formally introduced. It was not polite just to intrude on the young woman who was obviously busy contributing to the festival. By mid-afternoon, he was desperate, still not having found a friend who could negotiate the introductions. Time was running out. On his next break, he made his way to the fruit stall and confronted my mother before he had decided what excuse he would use for accosting her.

He was cornered. Recovering, he moved his hand in the general direction of my mother's apron at bosom height and said the first thing that occurred to him. "You really have some lovely melons!" Then he stopped and blushed, as he realized what his remark might have meant! He fled.

My mother did not understand what had happened, but she was surprised at the remark and the swift disappearance of the violin player. My Dad went back to the orchestra and was teased unmercifully for his ineptitude. He felt heartsick and also felt like a fool. He was definitely not going to try again. The other members of the band gave my dad a terrible time, waving their hands and asking about the whereabouts of fruit (melons in particular!).

In the late afternoon, it was clear that the party was almost over. If my Dad did not make contact with my mother, then he would have no way of ever knowing how to find her in the vastness that was Lisbon. Nobody knew her. None of his friends had even seen her before. Where could she have been hiding?

Then, the bassoon player, fed up with my father's shyness, said that he was going to approach her and explain what had happened. After the last song was sung and the band was ready to leave, he did, in fact, go over to my mother and tell her about the ongoing drama, saying that my dad was too shy and embarrassed to meet her, in light of his idiotic remark. My mother giggled and was then taken to the bandstand, where she was formally introduced to my father. They talked for an hour. My mother agreed to see him in Lisbon and gave him her address. She also admitted that she loved to play the piano, but she failed to tell him that her piano was an old cloth with fictitious notes that was rolled up and kept in a drawer at night …

My father fell in love with my mother in short order and persuaded her to marry him within the first six months of their acquaintance. They schemed and made plans for their future, which always included leaving Portugal permanently. Unfortunately, my mother became seriously ill after contracting an obscure virus which attacked her throat with a vengeance. She spent several weeks in special ward that isolated those with serious communicable diseases. Nobody was allowed into the ward as a visitor until she had made a full recovery, and that took a while. Those were the days when antibiotics were unknown. My father was distraught. As soon as my mother was fit to travel, he bought a passage on a steamer. Mom and Dad had their honeymoon on that ship on the way to Cape Town in South Africa. My father had contacts there in the form of friends who played in an orchestra. Soon, he was living a subsistence existence but enjoying every moment of exploring this great new land. He was happy just to see the new sights and did not want to make too many permanent commitments at that stage. My parents made their way north and ended up in Johannesburg eventually, where my pregnant mother gave birth to me in the house of an Italian woman, who had become a family friend.

After my birth, my mother decided that it would be wonderful to have her mother join the family. My grandmother Bicha was delighted to come out to the new land, so far removed from the sights and sounds of Lisbon, not only because she, too, wanted to see the world, but also because there was now an incentive in the form of a small wailing girl with blonde curls – her first grandchild.

My father had no difficulty finding work. Soon, we moved into an apartment near the huge Joubert park, in Johannesburg, where I had days playing in the sandpits and swinging from metal rings.

My father had had good connections back home in Portugal. His father was a well-known pharmacist who owned a large building – on one of the most prominent boulevards in Lisbon – in which he lived and in which the pharmacy was located. He had a family of two boys and two girls. My uncle had studied to be a chemist and helped out at the pharmacy, but he soon married. After a while, his wife persuaded him to accompany her and her sister, who was married to a fat, tubby soldier, a Lieutenant Colonel, who had very solid credentials and who had been appointed as the Governor General of Mozambique,(Portuguese East Africa). My father, who had spent his time in South Africa, was itching to make contact with his brother Antonio. To this end, we all departed for the Portuguese territory and the city of Lourenzo Marques, the capital of the colony of Mozambique, to meet our newly arrived relatives. I was just seven years old and had never met any of my relatives, so I thought that it would be a wonderful adventure. I was petted and spoiled, as the only child among all the adults, and was driven around in a chauffeured limousine. The Governor General was Paulo Rego. He used to invite me to go with him (alone in the official state limousine, with a smashing chauffer all dressed up in navy uniform with gold trim) to a beach restaurant, where we would stop and, with all the pomp, go and gorge ourselves on handmade gourmet ice cream! I also recall disgracing myself at the age of seven and throwing up all over the back seat and onto the plush navy blue carpeting, barely missing the most important and distinguished person in this huge land! I recall being dressed in uncomfortable smocked pink organdie creations in the breath-taking heat of the Mozambican summer!

Dad continued to play his violin at every opportunity and joined the Symphony Orchestra in Johannesburg, but he came to the conclusion that he needed to find more steady employment now that he had the family residing in Johannesburg on a permanent basis. He found employment in the offices of the Portuguese Consulate as assistant to the consul. He soon learnt the ropes. Again because of his impeccable character, pleasant and easy-going manner, and family connections back home, he soon took over and ran the entire office. He was so well liked that he remained the man to see when one visited the Portuguese Consulate General in Johannesburg. There was a consul, but he had only a diplomatic function. Each consul stayed only for a couple of years before being rotated out from the capital city of Pretoria, but my father remained as a permanent fixture and maintained continuity in the largest Portuguese consulate in Southern Africa, in the booming city of Johannesburg. He remained at his post until he died at the age of sixty.

We had occasion to do some sightseeing as well as some exploring of the new surroundings when we first arrived. When these moments came, we went off as a family, eager to see more of this exciting continent where adventure lurked around every corner. Everything was different from the European country to which my family had been accustomed. Adventure appeared even during the most prosaic outings. We encountered astounding episodes as we ventured further afield.

RHODESIAN INTERLUDE

Poised on the archaic crags and ridges of the Matopos Hills, which had formerly been the capital of the Matabele Tribes Empire, was Bulawayo City. Its impi warriors had lived in Kraals, which was filled with smoky fires, and kept their cattle close.

Here, once, King Lobengula had had dreams of greatness, before he suffered an ignominious defeat at the hands of the British. Today, this land is no longer a colony of the British Empire. It is an independent country called Zimbabwe.

The old dreams were replaced with those of the conquering British in their quest for empire, which was so ably aided by Cecil John Rhodes, who had been a lion among men and who wanted to be buried in these beautiful Matopos Hills with their far vistas of the land he loved, on the continent he had striven to "make pink" on the map. (All British possessions were painted pink on maps. In the past, all of India was coloured pink.)

Bulawayo continued to be a whitewashed British colonial city in those early days. It had a forced prettiness from carefully planted gardens, which included flowers from other continents, carefully tended and superimposed on the dry and unforgiving savannah.

It was, nonetheless, an exceedingly dull town for all that. Its only beauty was in the well-laid public parks that filled the city with well-tended flowers and serene expanses of grass.

My father had moved our family to Bulawayo from Johannesburg for a period of six months, on consular business. At first, he dallied with the idea of leaving the family behind, but my mother would have none of it, so, once more, he rallied his Model T Ford with the dickey seat. My mother, my grandmother, and I (aged seven) were packed into the vehicle, together with most of our belongings in the form of mounds of luggage.

My father thought of renting a small apartment, but it was impossible to rent a furnished one. Those with furniture were quite expensive, but the contents were definitely not up to snuff. He finally decided to continue to stay in the hotel into which we had first wandered when we arrived. It was out of the busy centre and out of the way. Also, it was located in front of a grandiose building with columns and turrets and a beautifully laid-out formal garden. We were so impressed at the time that we didn't realize that the building we so admired was one that was engaged in the brisk mortuary business and served as an undertaker parlour.

We had two interconnected rooms, one for my parents and the other for me and my grandmother Bicha.

Two days after our arrival, I caught measles and was quite ill. I was placed in quarantine, and Bicha looked after me. To our horror, Bicha, who could not remember that far back into her childhood and presumed that she had had the disease in her early life, quickly discovered that, in fact, she caught the inconvenient infection. Only she was very much sicker than I had been. My mother moved in with us and looked after our needs. My father was away all day so that when he came home, he was virtually alone and could only talk to us through the interconnecting door. It was a miserable time. Little did we know that things were only going to go from bad to worse.

Frankly, my mother was bored to death. When Bicha and I were napping in the afternoons, she snuck out of the rear of the hotel for some air and a short walk. There was normally nobody around, and she would go and sit under a tree. She looked over at the street traffic and noticed that everyone was riding bicycles. Bulawayo is exceptionally flat, so cycling was smooth sailing, if I may mix metaphors.

She discussed the idea of getting a bike with my father. He thought it was a good decision, especially as my mother had never learnt to ride as child and had always wanted to do so. She could spend her time learning in the walled back enclosure of the hotel.

It was a wonderful idea! She was thrilled at the prospect. That evening, my father brought home a second-hand bike for her to try her out her legs and balance.

Every spare moment when her charges were sleeping, my mother raced out to the back, retrieved the bike, and practiced her skills. It was very slow-going. Whenever anyone approached, she was too shy to go on. In any case, she was mindful of those of us quarantined at home.

She seemed not to realize that the bike had brakes and so used her feet to brake. She was finally getting the hang of bike riding and was thrilled to death. She wanted to show my father her newly acquired skills. When he arrived home one evening, she took him down to the yard to show off. Doing quite well, and with my father's encouragement, she went a little faster than usual. She tried to use her feet to stop, but when this did not help, she extended her leg towards a pile of lumber next to the wall of the kitchen. Then she gave a scream of pain when a rusted nail perforated her leg below the knee and the momentum made the nail came out the back of her leg. She certainly had stopped suddenly, but it took three people from the kitchen to extricate her from the woodpile, untangling her leg that had been badly perforated and had bloody entry and exit wounds.

Once again, the doctor had to come to see to our family. We were three down, and only my father was ambulatory. He had his days cut out for him. He had to go to work as usual. My mother was no longer able to look after the other invalids. We had to hire a nanny for the sickroom, and my dad had to come home from work and tend to my mother. She was hardly able to move. Going to the toilet was a major excursion.

I do recall, however, that we were endlessly entertained as we looked out of our bedroom windows. It was better than television. Daily, we saw well-attended processions of grieving relatives, hearses with mounds of flowers, and parades of impeccably groomed friends all in large flamboyant hats. We watched all the comings and goings, made conjectures about the deceased, and generally had a hilarious time looking at the solemn ceremonies getting underway, framed by our windows.

Those were depressing days; there were only sulpha drugs for my mother's wound, as penicillin had not yet been invented. It took some time for the wound to heal, as it had become infected. Her leg swelled to twice its size.

By the time we were all fit and well, it was almost time to go home again, back to South Africa.

Before we departed, we did go to the Matopos Hills to visit Cecil Rhodes's grave. He was the man who had had dreams for the Africa of the future and loved this land passionately.

Rhodes's grave is comprised of a flat stone about twelve feet long, laid horizontally on the ground with the inscription on a solid metal inlay about six to eight feet in diameter honouring Cecil John Rhodes. I have a picture of myself sitting on the edge of the background stone with my legs curled up, looking pleased with myself for having got over the measles and having finally been let out into the fresh air.

My mother's healing took quite a while. She spent the rest of her days with a huge, ugly scar on her calf below the knee. It took her a while to walk, and she never tried to ride a bike again. The scar was a permanent reminder of our funeral-watching Rhodesian sojourn.

THE PLAGUE

My father was going to Cape Town for a period of six months, and my mother insisted that the entire family go along for the trip. A hectic month followed in which both my grandmother and my mother attempted to put all our necessities into cardboard boxes and our clothes into four suitcases. There were dress rehearsals in which the Model T Ford with the dickey seat was packed and repacked, in order to squeeze not only the four of us, but also the innumerable little boxes, into every nook and cranny. It was a very tight fit when I finally climbed onto my grandmother's lap, into a small area behind the driver's seat.

There was stuff everywhere, and the dickey seat was filled to overflowing with the large suitcases, which were covered, for good measure, in a green and yellow cotton chenille bedspread. My mother had a gallon jug of water at her feet, as well as a variety of small shoeboxes tucked into awkward places next to her body.

We set off at dawn, in the twilight of the morning. I was groggy with sleep, so I curled up on my grandmother's lap and went on sleeping as if the journey was just a minor inconvenience.

Once out of the city and into the countryside, my mother was to get out of the car and open the farm gates that blocked the main highway. These gates were placed over steel rods with foot-long gaps in between them, making them difficult for pedestrians to manoeuvre. The idea was to prevent cattle from straying from one property to another. Large and often rusty signs indicated the dire consequences and penalties for not closing the gates after one went through.

Mom would slide out from under the boxes, trying not to displace the arrangements, and advance on the gate with a fierce look of determination in her eye and a knobkerrie in her hand. My dad would drive through the crossing grid, which made the car rattle in protest, and wait for my mom to shut the gate once again and then slide back in among the boxes.

The scenery was mostly dry and flat veld. After the second day of travelling, we arrived in the desert landscape of Northern Karoo. The land was only sparsely populated and was occupied by the Bushmen, a tribe of very small black people who were racially unlike any of the black tribes who inhabited South Africa. They were an ancient people with high cheekbones and slender stature. They did not wear garments of any kind except for animal pelts around the waist. These small people were nomadic and hunted with poisonous bows and arrows.

They did not build permanent huts but, rather, placed skins over a few sticks bent into the ground, the resulting "tents" providing shelter for the night. These people all seemed to have very loose skin around their stomachs, and the older women, in particular, had enormous folds drooping over their belts. I had been told that this was due to a feast-or-famine regimen. The Bushmen would starve for days and then, when the hunters came home with a successful catch, gorge themselves until none of the meat remained. I presume that this was because their food would otherwise readily deteriorate in the heat of the desert. So, it was customary to eat as much as possible at one sitting. They would become almost comatose at these meals, sometimes even achieving trance states. Then they would sleep for days, sprouting enormously engorged stomachs. They carried with them leather thong belts. As they went about their daily lives, they tightened the belts and pulled the loose skin closer into their waists. They travelled in small family groups. When we happened to see them, we stopped and looked at them with curiosity, but they showed no signs of friendliness. They would stop in their tracks and stare at us. Once they had seen enough, they departed after turning their backs on us as if we were not of much interest.

My father explained that a group of Bushmen had been coerced and bribed to be part of the South African International Exhibition of 1936, held in Johannesburg, where they were exposed to the ogling eyes of tourists. When asked what impressed them most about civilization, the Bushmen replied that water flowing out of a tap was the most magical sight of all!

My Mother hated the job of opening and shutting the gates, as, sometimes, farm dogs would appear and snarl at her heels, protecting their property. She had to beat a hasty retreat while we were momentarily besieged. Mom would wave her knobkerrie and attempt to intimidate the animals, but it was a false manoeuver, as she was terrified of hurting the dogs, even while she was making threatening noises and feints at the attackers.

Once, a gaggle of ostriches took over a gate crossing and peered at us territorially with their tiny eyes and a stupid expression. We were at a loss when wondering why they were threatening us. There was no food for them anywhere in this barren patch of earth, and the gate could not have been of much interest. Still, they moved about and strutted, shuffled, and threw the dust up into the air by scraping their feet on the ground. Spreading and then retracting their wings, they looked menacing. They were a sorry-looking bunch of birds. Their feathers were bedraggled and broken, most of the plumes of a dirty grey colour. These were wild ostriches that roamed the Karoo and the Kalahari. Those that were farmed were kept in clean enclosures and given food and vitamins to enhance their feathers, which were then much in demand on world markets.

We were kept at bay for about twenty minutes while we met angry shuffles and indignant stares. Then, as if summoned by an invisible hand, the ostriches stopped dead in their tracks, shuffled their feathers, and departed in precipitous haste in one direction, running at great speed and then disappearing behind some distant bushes, as if they had suddenly remembered something momentous that they had forgotten to do.

On the third day, the sun shone brightly and the air was hot and still. I removed my socks and shoes and sat happily singing in the back seat, eating a boxed lunch. Suddenly, the sunshine disappeared and, little by little, the sky darkened like this was a magical twilight. Where had the sun gone? We noticed that behind us was an enormous black cloud. As it approached and fell upon us, we were bombarded by millions of flying brown locusts. Father shut the windows and was trying to drive as fast as he could from the black portent of disaster.

The road was no longer visible: insects were coming in through a crack in the window left open against the stifling heat. Fluttering bodies flew around the inside of the car. I screamed. My grandmother retrieved her fly swatter and stoically swatted the offending intruders. Father drove on with accelerating speed, trying to outrun the swarms. Then, suddenly, the car came to a grinding halt and refused to start up again. My dad was not in the mood to climb out and rectify the problem. We sat as if imprisoned in the gloom, besieged by the billions of flying bodies that smacked onto the metal of the car and left entrails on the windows, smeared like blobs of sickly pus. I looked out the rear window and there, where our tyres had pressed on the dirt, were black smudges of dead bodies ground into the dust of the road.

We did not speak. We gazed in astonishment at the scene. The movements of the swarms were erratic. They travelled in waves and did not seem coordinated to go anywhere. Instead, the brown sea of fluttering bodies seemed in a state of flux. They did not follow any pattern. As soon as one wave was airborne, another, in a restless quiver, took its place on the veld. Suddenly, masses of bodies would alight on the car, and the interior would become as dark as night. Then, for no rhyme or reason, off they would go, careening into the distance as if their migration was being orchestrated offstage by an unseen mad maestro! My grandmother was making grunts in the back seat with every flying body she smashed with the trusty fly swatter. Indeed, she had a look of satisfaction on her face. This was more satisfying than tilting at windmills!

It was stifling hot in the car; there was no air. There seemed to be no end to our siege. About an hour later, we were still immobilized, parked on the roadside, being bombarded by wave upon wave of flying brown insects. My Mom had a headache, and I was close to tears, thinking that we would never escape from this inferno. Then, as rapidly as the locusts had arrived, they started to take flight and depart. The thick waves started to veer south and were joined by other, smaller waves. Smaller groups on the road surface started leaving, going in the same direction. Soon, there were only patches of solitary bodies flying hither and thither, entangled in the short grass and, I suspect, injured during their assault on our vehicle.

We hastily opened the car windows and doors, relieved that our tormentors had finally departed. Dad looked under the hood. The car was a mess. The radiator was encrusted with a thick brown ooze. The rest of the engine had not fared well, either. Dad, who was more inclined to playing string instruments than fiddling with errant car engines, decided that he was not up to the task of finding the problem and so started to look around for help. In the distance, he spotted lights emanating from a farmhouse. He set off at once and, as I recall, as he walked along, his steps were marked by the crunching of dead locusts underfoot. He disappeared into the gloom, only to return a while later with a strange assortment of helpers. There was a farmer, a large guy with a handlebar moustache and a slouch hat, followed closely by two tall African helpers, somewhat scantily dressed, and an assortment of black children of varying sizes and shapes all hungrily running along and looking for new excitement in their day. As if the locusts had not been enough! This motley crowd was followed by two large oxen which were dragging their feet and looking at us with sheepish expressions. They were being coaxed forward by a very small African man with an enormously long whip. I could hear the cracking of the whip as they approached. At first, I had thought that the oxen were being punished, but I learnt that, in fact, the whip was being cracked menacingly over their heads, not touching them at all. It was a reminder to the oxen to keep going forward.

The men soon had the car tethered from the front bumper and we passengers all made a hasty retreat. But two of the men had to go back to the kraal to fetch yet another unwilling ox before the vehicle would budge. Finally, when the car was tethered to three oxen, Dad climbed behind the wheel. My mother and grandmother and I walked beside him in a bedraggled procession towards the farmhouse.

We came to a halt beside a huge overhanging *stoep* covered in a tin roof and were invited to enter. Soon, the lady of the house, Mrs Coetzee, a large women wearing a long cotton dress and, on her head, a bonnet, showered us with hospitality, warm cups of steaming coffee, slabs of freshly baked bread, and apricot jam. Mrs Coetzee spoke no English, and none of us spoke Afrikaans, so communication was difficult; but my grandmother resolved the impasse by smiling and getting up to do the dishes. There was instant rapport. My dad was taken to the back shed to clean up.

Despite the best efforts of all the men, who had taken turns cleaning and fiddling with the engine, the car refused to start. Mr Coetzee invited us to sleep the night, as we could not go anywhere, and offered to ride over in the morning to his neighbour, who was a mechanic and who would, no doubt, solve the mystery of why the car refused to start.

We were ushered into a guest bedroom which had a large double bed and an even larger overstuffed sofa with a floral cretonne cover. The stuffing protruded in places. There was a jug and a basin of water on a wooden washstand. We made the best of a quick clean-up with the red Lifebuoy soap (which smelt of disinfectant), and then Dad lay down fully clothed on one side of the bed and slept the sleep of the utterly exhausted. My Mom undressed and, clad only in her slip, slid under the covers, and Gran made herself comfortable on the sofa, clutching me to her bosom. I was soon asleep, her comforting arms encircling me. At some time in the middle of the night, my mom arose and, with her shoe in hand, began smacking the wall vigorously.

"What on earth are you doing?" asked my dad.

"I have been bitten all over! Look at all the red marks on my arms and neck!" she said as she continued the assault on the wall. "Get up. Get up!" she yelled. "There are bugs on the walls!"

My father said nothing. He merely shifted his position from the bed to a straight chair next to a small table, put his head down on his arms, and continued to snore. Occasionally, he would peer at the wall in front of him and at the row of little brown specks that paraded down it. My grandmother got out her fly swatter and proceeded, with great gusto, to take swipes at the offending small reddish specks on the sofa. I slept on, unconcerned.

In the morning, Dad was up with the crow of the barnyard cock. He carefully took off his clothes piece by piece and shook them vigorously before dressing himself again. My mother looked a little worse for wear and continued to scratch at the bites on her neck. It took several weeks for the red splotches to disappear.

We had a good breakfast of eggs and sausages and more hot coffee, and my dad offered to pay the farmer for his hospitality. He refused, so he went out to the car and brought back a large box with canned goods and some fresh fruit and gave it all to Mrs Coetzee, with our thanks for their hospitality. Mr Coetzee then rode off rapidly on his horse to fetch the mechanic. Within an hour, our car was in starting order. We hugged the Coetzees and thanked them for all their help.

The car was still a mess. The yellow scum from the dead locusts was almost impossible to remove, so we, a sorry sight, limped into Cape Town.

Years later, when I was at the university, I met the professor who had, in fact, found the specific location and the place of origin of the locusts that had caused so much damage to so many African countries, as they ate everything in their path from north to south. The breeding grounds were found in an obscure corner of Egypt. Measures were then taken to destroy the locusts before they could turn into swarms and do more damage to crops in some of the poorest nations of Africa.

I remember parts of this episode in my life quite clearly, and I filled in the details from later conversations I had with my parents. The day of our plagues reminded me of biblical stories. I have never forgotten those days, so long ago, when I was only seven years old and when I experienced the swarms of locusts from Egypt.

GROWING UP A GIRL FOREIGNER

It is the experience of children who are fortunate enough to be brought up in a foreign country to, over time, understand, meld into, and become part of the new cultural experience. In my case, assimilation and belonging was never going to be an option. I was aware of a splintered reality.

Growing up as a small child exposed to the mélange of different cultures evident in South Africa was, for me, a very confusing experience. First and foremost, I had experience with other languages. There was the guttural Afrikaans, spoken as if slurred and often mixed with Shangaan or Xhosa – and, in the case of my Nanny, Zulu. There were the mellifluous tones of Portuguese juxtaposed with the clicking sounds of Xhosa.

It is one thing to be brought up as a monoglot in a particular culture, and quite another to speak one language at home (Portuguese), speak another language outside of school (English), learn a third as a spoken language (Afrikaans), study eight years of a dead language (Latin), and then go home and be accosted by the Xhosa clicks of my beloved nanny.

For me to think in terms of a "fixed self" was widely illusory. To be buffeted by the winds of many differing perspectives was as valuable a lesson as could be learnt anywhere. It was a soul-expanding experience.

Culture can be viewed as a lens through which one sees the world. Those who grew up amid conflicting cultural values and survived the experience have, in fact, traversed shark-infested waters and inherited an invaluable multicultural view of life. These people are able to see the more obscure details and colourations of their encounters and also better explain their experiences.

Taking nothing for granted became a given for me. Looking at the set of values and meaningless rituals from an old religion was difficult. The Ten Commandments seemed out of date. The coveting of one's neighbour's wife was puzzling. As to the coveting of one's neighbour's goods – was that not the basic tenet of capitalism?

I was prone to asking awkward questions.

"What language had been spoken by Adam and Eve?" I once asked a befuddled priest.

My father despaired, sighed, and wished that I had been born the boy he had so earnestly desired. I was hurt and decided early on to be *the best girl,* a girl who could be and do all the things my father had wanted of a son. I knew that I had to make my own way. No dressy dolls for me.

Meccano sets were more to my liking. I dressed in dungarees and was happy. I set a tight course to disprove my father's bias. My values were subject to seismic shifts, but I worked out the path I was to follow as I grew up, often trying to adhere to values that my parents thought strange.

I was not interested in playing with little girls. Their games were of little interest, and I considered them incalculably boring. What was the point in playing with a Shirley Temple doll? It just sat there. But assembling a plane that could then fly on the lawn was infinitely intriguing.

My father was mystified and sent me mixed messages, often glancing at me in disapproval. But when I went to school when I was nine, I was determined to make my father proud. I achieved above-average grades, which gained my father's respect. I did, in any event, enjoy playing with boys. While we were living in Cape Town, I had a great time enjoying the company of no fewer than three little boys who lived in the townhouse next to ours and whose father was a dentist. We were fortunate that our abodes were situated in front of a national park; as children, we had merely to cross the road to enter a wonderland forest, replete with huge fallen logs that we could climb. Every day, we would play hide-and-seek and Ali Baba and the Forty Thieves, during which we hid treasures which others tried to find among the foliage. On one occasion, I had an unusual experience. I had noticed that two of the boys were adjusting their trouser legs and then watering the holes in the log so as to make small puddles. *What a fun thing to do,* I thought; it would never have occurred to me to do such a thing! I tried to imitate the boys and readjusted my clothes in order to take better aim. What a disaster! All I achieved was wet socks, and I discovered that I was definitely not able to aim into the knot of the tree. I went home in disgust, with pants that were soaked. My grandmother kept insisting that I should have come home as soon I wanted to go to the toilet and not left things to the last moment. She had no clue that I had wanted to imitate the boys but had not succeeded. I felt that I had something missing. Exactly what, I had no idea, but the episode disturbed me considerably. Many years later, during my training as a psychologist, I realized that I had developed the female castration complex. I vividly recall how the experience of trying to urinate into the tree hole shaped my vision of myself as having something lacking – because I was a girl!

THE POLITICAL CLIMATE AND THE RISE OF APARTHEID IN SOUTH AFRICA

Living and growing up in South Africa was a study in contrasts. In this remarkably beautiful land with as diverse a population as could be found anywhere, the social divides were actually abysses. There were a scant two million Caucasians in a sea of twenty-five million Africans, mainly called Bantu. But this does not give a true picture of the diversity. There were innumerable tribes and sub-tribes, each with their own language and complex social structure. There was, in addition, a swelling population of displaced peoples who had come from other regions and remote villages (such as Mozambique) and resettled near the gold mines in the Witwatersrand, with the promise of instant riches in return for hard labour. These men were often innocents abroad who were separated from their families for years at a time. They had harsh contracts to fulfil. After suffering intense culture shock when they first arrived on the train platforms in the centre of Johannesburg, they were housed in men's dormitories. They may have lived tribal lives in remote corners of Mozambique, but those lives had been free from oppression and racial discrimination. In those remote villages was none of the intense racial hatred engendered by the South African system of apartheid.

The Portuguese had a benevolent and paternalistic approach to native peoples, which was in evidence as I was growing up. At the time, any Mozambican African who wished to be integrated into the European society and claim full rights of citizenship needed to fulfil several criteria. He had to be able to read and write at a grade-four level, be a Christian, and fulfil the ordinary citizen's duty of submitting to military conscription and training. He was allowed to marry only one wife. There was also the matter of paying taxes as a full-fledged citizen. Most preferred to remain in their villages, live under tribal law, and marry as many wives as their finances would allow. (Women were acquired as wives through the payment of *labola,* which was generally a gift of several cows given to the bride's father in exchange for his daughter.)

The Portuguese administration appointed several bush advocates who would sit with the tribal councils in various designated areas see that justice in disputes was dispensed fairly and not arbitrarily, as had often been the case in the past.

My father was not directly involved with the welfare of tribal Portuguese citizens, as there was a Portuguese Department of Native Affairs which dealt with them. But I do remember that once a year we were invited to the natives' annual celebration. A cow was slaughtered and roasted on an open spit while several tribes demonstrated their prowess in traditional warrior dances. These men were predominately Shangaans, and they had arrived with their batteries of marimbas, which emitted sweet tinkling sounds, and their magnificent choir of songs, sung in complicated unrehearsed descant which made my soul resonate.

My father was the representative of Portugal and, hence, also a representative of Mozambique. The Africans showed much respect towards him. At the end of the dancing and the jubilation, they shouted, "Long live Senhor Almeida Jorge," followed by, "Long live Portugal." Finally, as the finishing touch, they said, "Long live São João" (the patron saint of Lisbon, dead for four hundred years!).

My father had grave concerns about these men. They arrived almost like children from the bush into the hell of discontent that was South Africa. He feared for them. He was instrumental in arranging for their monies to be withheld until they were ready to return home. At first, it was customary for the men to be paid a lump sum for their hard work prior to their departure; but it was soon apparent that there were those scoundrels who were ready to take advantage of these tribal men's innocence and rapidly separate them from the money they had earned by the sweat of their brows. The labourers would depart on the trains to Komatipoort (on the border), laden with overpriced bicycles, gaudy shirts, and trinkets for their wives; toys for their children; and cheap radios. Many returned home penniless so that their families were worse off than when their men had left two years previously.

Over the years, a policy evolved to prevent these abuses, and so the larger portion of the earnings were kept back and delivered to the miners at the Portuguese border before they entered Mozambique at the last stop before they arrived home in Lourenzo Marques (now Maputo). This, at the very least, ensured that the men would arrive home with money in hand and that their families could benefit after having endured the hard separation.

In South Africa, the gulf between black and white was a yawning chasm, but there were tremendous gashes in the social fabric of the European population, as well. The new immigrants had definite ideas about the country. The large and affluent population of well-educated, English-speaking Jews was the last stronghold of liberal ideas. The Afrikaners, who considered themselves the inheritors of this patch of Earth, given their long struggles in the past, bitterly opposed this population. Their desire to maintain their distinct language and culture forged after long suffering on African soil in their initial encounters with the African tribes, and their later bitter defeat and dispossession by the British during the Boer War, had soured their perspectives. This was the land which had been given to them by God, and they were not going to share it with anyone.

Never was a small country so divided by race, tribe, ethnic origin, colour, language, and religion.

The white population, swelled by immigration from Europe after the Second World War, still only numbered a scant three million. In order to maintain a firm grip on the government, the land, and the major institutions, solutions were found which distanced, controlled, and beat down any ideas of self-expression in the twenty-five million black Africans.

The African population, itself a melting pot with great divides, had never been a cohesive group. The whites profited from this lack of cohesiveness when they divided and then ruled the native peoples. It was only when Mandela was released from prison that the African National Congress began to voice the collective demands of all Africans and make inroads against the apartheid regime that the Afrikaners and their Calvinist Dutch Reformed Church had put in place.

The public policy had evolved to separate black areas from so-called white areas, except for those people who might be useful to the white minority. Blacks were banned from living in the cities, where employment was to be found, and were sent into the impoverished Bantustans. These were predominantly rural areas with few resources and, more likely as not, no infrastructure. Whole families had been displaced into poverty. Often when the men returned to the cities seeking employment, they were caught by the police and placed in prison because they had no legal passes to permit them to seek work. It was a vicious circle. During this era, there was a huge rise in outlaw gang activity. Also, crime escalated. The laws promulgated had brought about undesired results, and the whites found themselves with a siege mentality. The different ethnic groups were segregated to their allotted Bantustans and told to "develop separately." The fact that there was no infrastructure, no schools, no medical facilities, and no employment did not seem to bother the government unduly. The repercussions for the black population were many. The women, especially those with young children, were left in exceedingly vulnerable situations, with no visible means of support and no opportunities for employment. In order to survive, they moved surreptitiously into the cities seeking work and ran afoul of the law. Many were picked up as criminals because they lacked passes; in consequence, they were separated from their children. Children were often separated from both their parents and left in the dubious care of elderly relatives in impecunious circumstances back in the Bantustans. There was a huge increase in poverty in rural areas and the destruction of families whose men were permanently displaced.

The Afrikaner population, with its extremist views, gained power, closed ranks, and proceeded to rule the country. South Africa had been part of the British Commonwealth, but suddenly, when the Afrikaners assumed power, they were confronted with the disapproval of the British Commonwealth members. A vote was taken. The last and deciding vote in favour of South Africa's being ousted from the group was cast by the Canadians.

This was the time when the dragons were unleashed. South Africa was like a rogue state. Most of the civilized world looked upon its policies with horror.

A MATTER OF INTEREST

The offices of the Portuguese consulate, in which both my parents worked, were situated opposite the main post office in central Johannesburg. On the twelfth floor of an elegant building, the offices themselves were fairly small for the demands of an increasingly burgeoning population of immigrants and for the demands of people and goods travelling between the Republic of South Africa and the colonies of Mozambique and Angola. The Consulate prepared the documents issued Visas and passports to those crossing in and out of Portuguese Territory.

On Saturday mornings, the crowds overflowed from the small waiting room onto the outside glassed-in corridor, as throngs of residents and tourists awaited the processing of their legal papers and the issuing of stamps and visas on their documents.

My mother performed several functions at once at the consulate. She was the official sworn translator, the office manager, the general factotum, and the person who ushered people into the inner sanctum, where my father had his office.

On this particular day, the Saturday crowd was particularly large. My mother was trying to expedite the requests of the people who were in the queue. A very tall man approached the window. He had kept the hat on his head and appeared to be ill at ease in what seemed to be new clothes. He demanded to speak to my father in person.

"What exactly is the nature of your business with Mr Jorge?" my mother enquired. The man said that he could not tell anyone and demanded again to speak to my father. My mother asked him to wait and returned to processing the huge pile of documents neatly piled on her desk. After a while, she went into my father's office with a large number of passports for signature and suddenly remembered that the tall man was still waiting in the entry hall for an audience with my dad. When all the documents had been signed and the consular stamps appended, my mother once more retrieved the pile and went out to summon the man to my father's presence.

The stranger shook hands with my father and proceeded to retrieve from his coat pockets several small bundles wrapped in brown paper and tied with string. He said nothing, but laid the parcels on the desk in front of him. My father, who was usually slightly distracted and pressured with so much to do, did not quite understand what was happening.

"I want you to keep all this in the safe for me until I return," the man said.

My father looked at the parcels and, at first, did not understand the request.

"I am going back to Madeira. My mother found me a bride, and I married her last week by proxy. Next week, I am going home to fetch my new wife, and I shall be away about six months. I want you to keep all my money. After all, you have a big safe in the consulate, and you are the only one I can trust to look after what is mine."

My father explained that he could not be responsible for the care of private funds and suggested that the man open a bank account. "I can go with you and help you, if you like," he said.

The man was now angry, and he refused to even talk about opening an account into which he could put his hard-earned cash. He explained that the government was only out to get his cash and that the banks were no better After all, he said, my father had a reputation for scrupulous honesty and, in any case, was the representative of Portugal. But best of all, he had access to a large safe …

"The money in the safe belongs to the State, and as such I cannot place other monies in that safe. It would not be allowed. It would be a contravention of the law." My father continued to offer alternatives for the placement of the man's money. "What about the post office or the building society?" he asked.

The man was now visibly agitated, angrier, and more insistent by the moment. The office was getting more and more crowded, and no work was being done. The man refused to budge. He became angry and even threatening, claiming that my father, as the representative of the only people he trusted, had to look after his money in his time of need. My father was desperate to resolve the situation and to get rid of the man. The stranger suddenly got up, straightened his hat, opened the door, and abruptly left.

There on the desk was a fortune.

Dad called a friend and a confidante, a certain Mr Cohen, and explained his dilemma. There in front of him were the eight or nine packets of money. My dad and Mr Cohen sat down and started to count the cash. There was over thirty thousand rand – a considerable amount of money even in those days. Then the consular courier was summoned and the money placed in his bag. The three men went off to the bank around the corner. My father insisted that Mr Cohen co-sign the account so that if anything went wrong, there were two people who were aware of the circumstances and knew to whom the money belonged.

Eight months went by. My father had almost forgotten the episode with the crush of daily living. The money sat in the bank earning interest till, one day, the stranger in the hat returned.

It was another busy Saturday morning. The man came to the window and asked to speak to my father. He introduced his new wife, a shy, attractive woman much younger in age than he.

My mother stalled, knowing the story of the packets of money. "Actually, the safe is closed for today," she said. "Can you come back on Monday and perhaps bring a bag?"

At first, it seemed that there might be problems, but the man wanted to appear serene in the presence of his new wife. He readily agreed.

On Monday, there was scramble to the bank to close the account and collect the cash. But there were problems. In the first place, the bank wanted to issue a cashier's cheque. In light of the circumstances, this would have let the cat out of the bag. Some cash was obtained, but it took hours of going to other banks to gather the sum needed. It took almost the entire Monday. My father, who hated conflict, was almost on the verge of declaring his duplicity when, finally, the full amount appeared in the consular courier bag. He counted and collated it with a sigh of relief.

Near the end of the day, my father placed the box in the back of the consular safe and awaited the return of the man from Madeira. He arrived almost at closing time, and my father ushered him into the inner sanctum and produced the box in which the neat piles of cash were arranged. The Madeiran looked suspiciously at the lack of brown paper and string on the bundles and was preparing to leave when my father made him sit down and count each bundle, signing a document saying that they had all been received and the amounts were correct.

"I did not actually ever count how much there was in the bundles," the Madeiran said. "I just kept adding to the piles as I worked my vegetable farm. I saved so I could have enough for a wife!"

But that was not the end of the story. There was another problem looming on the horizon. The bank retained a rather large lump sum in the form of interest on the monies banked, and its officers sent a letter enquiring whether these should be reinvested. This was another dilemma for my father until my mom came up with a brilliant idea. She proposed phoning the Madeiran's wife and asking her to come to the consulate on a weekday when her husband was working.

The new bride agreed to come. My mother then took her out for coffee and told her that the consular services had a problem in that, because of her husband's insistence, the monies left at the consulate had, in fact, not been placed in the safe, as her husband had supposed, but had been gathering interest in the bank. My father did not want to tell the Madeiran that he had been hoodwinked, but, by the same token, he could not keep monies that were not his. My mom proposed that the Madeiran's wife be given access to the interest monies, but only if she promised not to breathe a word of the deception. She was stunned at the revelation, but she agreed.

And so it was that, that afternoon, the Madeiran's wife received access to a substantial sum of money, legitimately hers, which could give her some freedom to manoeuvre in her life. She had come from a poor family, so the money seemed to her to be an absolute fortune. She was ecstatic and would call my mother over the years to thank her for the brilliant idea. My mom believed in women's rights and freedoms, anyway.

It was a lifetime later, after my father had died suddenly, that my mother was approached by a woman at Dad's funeral. She appeared familiar, but who she was, Mom could not recall on the spur of the moment. She spoke to my mother after the funeral and offered her condolences, proceeding to tell her that the cash that my mother had given her on the occasion of her marriage so long ago (and which her husband had never known about) had proved an invaluable resource in her life. She hugged my mother and thanked her for her resourcefulness and kindness in providing her with a nest egg which had made an incalculable difference to her in the course of her life.

EARLY DAYS

I read the evening papers before my father got home and was dimly aware that there was a large conflict unfolding. As the time dragged on, I took it for granted that the war was always in the background in the panorama of our lives. I became adept at knitting socks for sailors, in thick waterproof wools, and was able to turn a neat heel. My mother organized concerts where those people who belonged to nations not actually involved in the war were discreetly co-opted into providing elaborate national costumes and training their youth for national dances. Proceeds were donated to the war effort. This was all fun and games. I was bedecked in a Minho costume and learnt to dance Portuguese National dances.

Then, one Saturday afternoon, I went with my mother and grandmother to the train station. We were there with groups of women to welcome the wounded who had come down for treatment and those who came for R & R, weary from battling Rommel's panzer force in the North African deserts. Apart from the South Africans who were returning home, there were Italian prisoners of war and Australians and New Zealanders who were looking for fun and games, mainly searching for the nearest pub in which to drown their sorrows and celebrate their victories.

Suddenly, the horror of the war began to dawn on me. There were stretcher cases of horribly mutilated men. There were those without eyes and limbs, and sad cases of those who looked vacant and unheeding – and deeply hurt in their souls. I went home crying.

Baragwaneth Hospital was overflowing. The South African medical establishment did us proud. The only note of dissent was from the Ossewabrandwag. This was a group of diehard anti-English Afrikaners who, in their zeal, had decided to beat up recruits and openly side with Hitler and adopt his fascist principles. The group was not large, but I was appalled at the vehemence with which its members attacked soldiers coming home from the war, denouncing them as traitors to the Afrikaner cause. Crime increased considerably during this period. Soldiers on leave could be found lying drunk in parks or fighting in the pubs. The Australians had fought hard and now drank equally hard and generally misbehaved to alleviate the months of tedium before redeployment. Nevertheless, the vast majority of the wounded were invited into homes and treated with kindness, respect, and gratitude.

My personal life was mundane, routine, and boring. Apart from my colleagues at school, I did not have many friends. I lived in the small apartment on Twist Street, continuing to share a room with my grandmother. I listened to the radio and was particularly taken with *The Adventures of the Scarlett Pimpernel.* I listened to the thrilling episodes when the aristocrats were rescued from the guillotine during the French Revolution. I read a great deal after I completed mountains of homework, conscientious of my school commitments. I detested sports and learnt to go week after week to the Saturday "detention" room to do extra schoolwork in Latin (Caesar's Gallic Wars) rather than muck about on a wet field chasing a field hockey ball. It took years for the nuns to finally unravel the mysteries of all those detentions. By that time, it was too late for me to join the team anyway. My Latin took a turn for the better!

My father decided that as I always had my nose in a book, I was not to be permitted to read anything on Sundays. I resolved this impasse and took up knitting. I made friends with the best knitter in the class, learnt all the tricks of the trade, and turned out gloves and socks with many a finely turned heel. As a result of this training, for most of my life I made all my sweaters. It was only when I got back to Canada in the 1960s that I deigned to purchase sweaters ready-made. To this day, I still have a large collection of finely knitted sweaters, all in different styles and patterns (Aran was my favourite).

Looking back now, I am aware that my upbringing set me on a course where I was always happy to be on my own. I did and still do enjoy solitude. This is not to say that I do not like people. I do. I find it very easy to relate to all kinds of people, and I am always intrigued by cultural differences. I look upon certain people I run across as conundrums to be unravelled slowly with acquaintanceship. I am generally observant, so this way of seeing the world helped me in my chosen career as a psychologist.

I continue to be an intensely private person. I do not do well at parties, and I find it hard to talk to people who are slightly under the weather and prattling on about things of little or no consequence. The fact that I do not drink probably exacerbates the situation. Frankly, I enjoy the handful of really close friends I have. They are all of long standing. My best friend has been just that for the best part of seventy years. Despite the fact that she lives in Cape Town and has not ever travelled anywhere, we have shared a lively correspondence over a lifetime.

REPRIEVE FROM A DULL LIFE

I had four school uniforms consisting of navy gyms, black knee-length bloomers, black stockings, and lace-up black shoes. White long-sleeved shirts were enlivened with a tie bearing the school colours. A navy blue blazer covered the uniform, and it had the regulation school colours on the breast pocket. A felt hat with the school hatband (or a panama hat in summer) alleviated the dreariness. Strict measure was taken as I grew up to see that female students' uniforms were always below the knee. We did gymnastics in our uniforms, as it was unseemly to show our legs to the male gym instructor, who, given his age of about eighty or so, would not have been even mildly interested in our legs – or any other part of our bodies, for that matter. But the nuns had to be sure that protocol and ladylike behaviour prevailed. The only concession was white gym shoes. If we arrived in the gym hall without them, then our instructor, who was German, would shout, "Why you come with your boots?" And we would pretend to be mortified!

For many years after I left school, I would not wear navy blue, and black lace-up shoes were anathema. I have nothing in my wardrobe that is navy blue, even today (except jeans!).

On weekends, I had two going-out dresses. When I came home from school, I changed into one or the other of my at-home dresses: modest cottons made by my grandmother. That was it! My entire wardrobe could have fit into a small suitcase. But I did not feel deprived. After all, I lived in a sea of deprivation that was hard to comprehend. All the black South Africans were so pitifully deprived that, in contrast, I felt that I needed for nothing.

In the last two years of school, I became a boarder. That meant sharing a small room with another girl, getting up every morning at 5.00 a.m. to attend Mass, and then having a quick breakfast, followed by an hour of study. The requirements for university entrance were quite strict. One had to pass English grammar, literature, poetry, and composition. Then there was to be one ancient and one modern language (in my case, Latin and Portuguese). The schools attended by boys chose to teach Greek instead of Latin. I am sure that, as a living language, Greek has its uses, whereas Latin, to me, seemed to have no earthly use at all. It was said that Latin is the basis of so many modern tongues and was therefore certainly useful, but, as I already spoke a Latin language at home, learning Latin at school seemed wasteful and redundant. I so hated Caesar's Gallic Wars!

World History was fun after learning about the dreadfully dull South African Kaffir Wars and the Voortrekkers! I chose to study the rise of Japan as an elective. We studied English history from the magna carta in great detail, as well as the rise of Germany and Italy – prophetic, as we were soon were to embark on the Second World War. Then there was biology (mainly botany) and mathematics – covering algebra and trigonometry. It was a heavy load, and I took my studies seriously. I had decided that I was going to fail Afrikaans, but I took Portuguese (grammar and literature) instead and came through it all with flying colours. We had to take one ancient and one modern language other than English to fulfil the requirements of the Cambridge University entrance exam.

I was seventeen and in white socks when I passed the finals exams and was accepted into the science programme at the University of the Witwatersrand. Looking back, I think I should have done languages and fine arts, but the choice was made and I embarked on the beginnings of my academic career with vim and vigour. At the tender age of seventeen, despite my short socks, I went right on having no social life in the accepted sense, spending all my time working hard to pass my exams.

When the war ended, the South African soldiers returning from the wearying battles against Rommel in the desert were give government grants to study if they had the qualifications. As a result, our classes were enormous. Our geology and palaeontology class had over three hundred students, only six of whom were women, me included, sitting terrified in the first row of seats in a temporary hut that had been erected to house the returned soldiers. The men, realizing our vulnerability, gave us women a hard time by whistling and catcalling.

As a class, we would go out in huge trucks on field trips into the countryside to look at rock formations. I would sit next to the driver in the front, as silent as the grave and still in my little white socks!

There were dances, of course, but I was too shy to venture out to these, especially as I had to have the young man come to my home to meet my parents and be scrutinized and drilled as some sort of person with evil intentions towards the only innocent daughter of my irate father. It was agonizing. One brave Jewish boy invited me to the Rag Ball, which was a *big deal!* I told him of my dilemma, and he chose to humour me and come and meet my parents.

He arrived innocently on a Saturday afternoon. Our servant, bedecked in a white starched coat, gave him tea and biscuits in the lounge. My grandmother was the conciliator and smiled sweetly, while my father grilled the poor boy about the ins and outs of the proposed ball.

"How will you get there?" asked my father.

"I will get a friend to drop us off," the boy replied.

"Not good enough," replied my father, "but it can easily be fixed. I will take my daughter and pick you up, and I will deliver you both to the auditorium." It was not a question; it was a command. The poor fellow had to accept the terms of the arrangement.

As if this was not bad enough, on the appointed day I got into my long dress and finery, and Dad took me in the front seat with him, my mother and my grandmother coming along for the ride. I was humiliated, but I persevered. The worst was still to come. We picked up my boyfriend from his parents' house and sat him next to my dad in the front seat.

I had a remarkably fun evening and danced the night away until, on the stroke of midnight, as with Cinderella, my father reappeared on the scene to look for me and tell me that it was about time for me to go home and for him to take my partner home, too.

I was completely humiliated and became the subject of many snide comments and giggles. My father did not understand that, by his actions, he was, in fact, besmirching my character. The other boys wondered what I was up to that required such careful supervision!

I went home, thanked my partner for his invitation, and decided then and there never again to go out under any circumstances, with anyone. It was just too hard. I was not prepared either to disobey my father or be ridiculed. I did the next best thing to having a social life: I spent all my time studying, with enviable results.

I did go away on vacation with my mother to stay with friends in what was then Lourenco Marques, the capital of Mozambique. I enjoyed the beach and my Portuguese friends. It was a time to enjoy some freedom from all the studies.

But apart from these rare episodes, my life continued with unmitigated sameness. On one occasion, I met an interesting man. He, much older than I, was the general manager of the Polana Hotel, the largest hotel in Mozambique at the time. I was terribly flattered by the attention. He then came to Johannesburg and called on my father. I was informed that he had requested to call on me, and I agreed to have lunch with him downtown (we ate cannelloni) – all with my father's blessing. The protocol was being observed.

The man's name was Armando. He was fourteen years my senior and gave the impression of being highly ethical and terribly hard-working. I spent a vacation with my mother in Lourenco Marques, and he insinuated himself on us both. He was charming, chivalrous, and soft-spoken. I met his parents. His father was ill and bedridden, and his mother was a kindly and self-sacrificing woman who seemed to have no other life than playing the role of servant to her family. In a snobby city, she was not accepted for many years as she had lived with Armando's father and only married him shortly before he died. I liked her almost immediately and felt a great deal of sympathy for her. She, in return, was endlessly kind to me, never wanted to intrude, and went to the ends of the earth to get anything I asked of her. She was simply one of the kindest human beings I had ever met. She had been born in Calabria and had come to Mozambique as a young girl. She still spoke Italian at home. Her Portuguese was only just understandable.

Armando asked my father for my hand in marriage. Not really understanding much of the situation, I agreed to marry him when he proposed. At least my life would be more exciting (or so I thought). I was going to complete my BSc degree and then marry. But things have a way of rearranging themselves. Fate intervened in the form of the infantile paralysis epidemic.

I came home from classes one day thinking that I might have the flu. A doctor came to examine me and made the dreaded diagnosis. Disinfectant swabbed on wet sheets was fixed to my door. Within hours, I was moved to a quarantine hospital in one of the suburbs. I was quite sick. On the second day, they put me in an iron lung. I was in that claustrophobic machine for four days, after which it seemed that my respiration improved enough for me to go back to the ward, where they placed a contraption that looked like a chicken-wire nest with bulbs of light inside it over my body to the waist. I steadily improved and then started to walk in what I perceived to be a weakened state. Finally, I walked out of the hospital and was told to take it easy!

I had no option. I had no hope at that point of making up for all my lost university studies and so I gave up, thinking that I would leave things for a time when I felt better. There was no reason for me not to marry when I fully recovered. This I did. The ceremony was held in the Catholic church, as it seemed important to my father and my future husband would think of no other option. I kept my ideas to myself and went along, with many misgivings.

During the signing of the documents in the presbytery of the church, my new husband shouted and rebuked me on a trivial matter. This sent a chill down my spine. He was showing his hand. But it was too late to go back on my word. I put on a good face and persevered.

Armando and I drove out of town to a hotel on a lake, but the wrong room had been booked so that we ended up without a view of the lake and with a view of the kitchen! My new husband did not think it important. He paid me no attention whatever. His first act was to call his father and tell him that all was over and that he would soon be home. He then lay down on the bed and fell asleep. I left the room and wandered into the garden. There, I cried and felt more alone than it is possible for a human being to feel in one day!

I was very innocent and became pregnant on my marriage night. The entire transaction was horrific for me. There was very little preamble. It was a case of "Shut up and let us get this over. After all, you know nothing about this, so leave it to me."

We left for Mozambique the next day by train. I tried valiantly not to notice the sanctimonious facade of my mate. I realized that beneath the surface lurked a very uneducated, perverse, authoritarian, and emotionally damaged individual. We had nothing to talk about. He resented any comments I made about the state of affairs in the colony. I was mad enough to make political commentary! He wanted a trophy, a young and attractive woman, to enhance his prestige. That was all I meant to him. My days were spent in shock. He had the hotel staff report to him on my whereabouts. I ventured to tell him that I had encountered a schoolmate from the university and was so happy to talk to him. "I know all about that," Armando said. (He had been spying on me!)

All the local women did was have "teas," in which they sat around and gossiped while the nannies looked after their children at home. I was utterly bored. I decided to learn French and, to this end, went twice weekly to visit a little old woman, a Parisian, who took great pride in her heritage but who, even after forty years in the province, spoke lamentable Portuguese.

I made friends with a local female doctor and finally got all the information I needed about unmentionable topics.

I returned to stay with my parents in Johannesburg, making the train journey back on my own a month before my baby girl was born. My husband was too tied up with work to be there for the birth, but he instructed his cousin Emma, who lived locally, to visit me in hospital and see how things were going. Two weeks later, I was on the train back to Lourenco Marques with my little bundle. I felt abandoned!

The baby was born with a red, squashed face and pitch-black hair about three inches long all over her head. She was, without doubt, the ugliest new-born I had ever seen. My father looked at her and made no comment. My mother said nothing, while my grandmother smiled and told me not to worry, as babies' first hair always falls out. The child was the spitting image of her father (at age forty!).

The nurses did their best. They even put a bow on an elastic as a topknot. Like that, my child looked like a Chinese doll. But she always wore a frown!

Armando was pleased as punch but hardly ever had anything to do with the baby. I had a nanny who looked after her while I went to the dining room for meals.

It was during these days that Amalia Roderigues, the Portuguese fadista (a singer of fados), visited. The entire pool was decorated in her honour. She sang from the deep end of the pool on a beautiful summer night, when the air was just soft as cotton wool and there was no background breeze coming in from the ocean. The place was crowded. I was fascinated by Amalia's charisma and skill as a singer. Fados are actually moaning lamentations over the sad state of a romance gone wrong or the fate of long-lost love. They are old and traditional. Once heard, they can never be forgotten. I recall that I had sat in a small wine shop once while visiting Lisbon and had heard a young woman enveloped in a black shawl singing fado and almost crying over a long-lost love and subsequent abandonment. Some in the audience were actually "happily crying"! A friend admitted that the Portuguese are only "happy" when they can identify with a tragedy.

Then there was news that the Aga Khan was coming to stay at the Polana Hotel. His wife was Rita Hayworth. We were all intrigued by her notoriety. Unfortunately, in Mombasa, her previous port of call, she had decided to leave her husband, so she did not grace us with her presence. There was the Aga Khan ball. I decided to make an organdie ball gown for myself. It turned out quite well. I had my dance with the prince, who was a handsome man but an unbelievable womanizer. We talked about his stables in Ireland and about horse racing, a topic about which I know absolutely nothing. He was certainly not heartbroken about Rita's departure and was having a whale of a time at the ball held in his honour. He flew back to London and immediately had an affair with an English model of some repute. The two died in a car accident shortly thereafter.

Then I learnt something that would drastically alter the course of my life. I learnt the truth about my sanctimonious husband. He had a dark past. He had a criminal record. He had beaten an African to death. I was stunned. I knew that I had only one path of action. I had to leave as soon as possible, and I had to take my baby with me. This was the last straw!

The law in Mozambique was primitive in the sense that, according to the statutes, the child of a marriage belongs to the husband. I was horrified. I could not tell anyone my well-guarded secret. I had been given the information in confidence. I only knew that I had to go as soon as possible. If life had been detestable before, it was unbearable now. I thought it best to say nothing until I got out of the country. I told my husband that I was going to go back to finish my degree. It seemed plausible. I booked the train journey, got authorization on my passport from my husband, and went back to Johannesburg and enrolled in the third year to attempt to complete the degree and pick up the shattered pieces of my life.

It was one of the hardest years of my life. Having to look after a small baby on my own, having very little money, and doing all the work required was an almost monumental task.

I rented a miniscule apartment in a very old building, enrolled at the university to finish my degree, and brought my small baby with me. I would take her to the university. While I was at classes, she was in the pram being wheeled around by a black nanny until I was free. In the afternoons, she slept under a huge tree while I was at the biology and chemistry labs. After four o'clock, I would again bundle her up and take the baby-laden tram home along with my books to spend the evening studying and then sleeping.

All was well when we were both feeling well, but, as things turned out, my baby was teething while I was studying for my finals. I was up nights pacing with a book in one hand and a whimpering baby in the nook of my other arm. I finally realized that I could no longer continue this way, so I approached my mother-in-law to collect her granddaughter at the airport just before I had my finals. I bundled up my little girl and took her out to the airport, where, like a parcel, she was delivered to the stewardess. Wrapped warmly and wearing a little white bonnet, she seemed to relish the adventure. It was but a short flight, and I knew that she was being delivered to someone who would have her best interests at heart. I was utterly exhausted, but at least now I was going to get a night's sleep!

My final exam was in genetics. We students were provided with a bottle of specially bred fruit flies (*Drosophila melanogaster*). We were to anaesthetize the flies and look at the mutations carefully and then see how we could account for their characteristics. It was fun. The only problem was that I had had a rough night with the baby. As a result, instead of placing an anaesthetic to keep the flies asleep while I examined their mutations, I opened the bottle and they all zoomed out happily into the examination room. The invigilators rushed to pull out their handkerchiefs and attempt to catch (but not kill) the errant *Drosophilae*. It was pandemonium! I did, however, take a good guess at the mutation. I am glad to report that I did quite well on the exam, despite all the distractions.

I went home and slept for almost forty-eight hours. Wild horses would not have awakened me. The next day, my mother and grandmother appeared, knocking on the door and waiting to ascertain whether I was dead or alive, as they had hardly seen me in the last few weeks. They took me out to a celebratory dinner, during which I misbehaved and giggled at everything, even if it could not have conceivably been construed as funny!

Then reality hit me. I knew I had to go back to Mozambique and organize the loose ends of my new life. I caught the train and travelled across the border to Lourenzo Marques in Mozambique, to the Polana Hotel where we lived permanently. It was a five star hotel facing the sea and on a Hill overlooking the ocean. We had a small suite and my husband was the General Manager. I knew that I would have to make serious plans. I was very excited to see my baby again. We spent our mornings at the huge hotel pool. I taught her to swim although she was so small, as I was terrified that she should one day accidentally fall into the water and drown. She was fearless. I had a whale of a time teaching her to dogpaddle. I have a photo of her in a two-piece swimsuit, sitting happily on the pool steps with a fat tummy protruding and two pigtails constraining the masses of dark brown hair. She had a frown as if seriously and studiously worried about the ills of the world she had come into and planning to set it to rights!

I had been stunned. For days, I barely functioned. What was I going to do? I was totally mortified and, worse, could confide in nobody, as I was just too ashamed. I was also angry. I was very angry, indeed. Armando had made me feel bad because I was not religious. Somehow, I was lacking: it was all my fault that I could not be loved. I was the one who did not fit in. I was flawed … but he had a murder conviction?

I finally decided that continuing a life with this man was too dreadful to contemplate. I was married to a man who had been tried and convicted of murder. I was going to leave Mozambique. I did not want to discuss the matter. Talking about his conviction was beyond the pale. I took my daughter and left.

Leaving my husband was not an easy matter. According to some archaic Portuguese law, children belong to the father. Since I was leaving him, I could not take my daughter across the border to the Transvaal without his permission. I knew that he would not give me the papers I wanted to get out of the country. I needed to have a strategy.

I alerted my parents to the state of affairs. As usual, my father came through for me. He put my daughter on my new Portuguese passport, which he issued through the Portuguese consulate (without my daughter's father's consent). One bright morning, I picked up my daughter, Maria Elena up from the sandbox and, with only a small case, took a taxi to the docks, where I bordered an Italian freighter called the *Spuma*. It usually took only ten passengers, but on this trip, I paid for a cabin and departed for Durban with a screaming child of three who yelled that she wanted to get back to her pool and sandbox!! We were the only passengers aboard.

It was only after the ship sailed that Armando realized that I had gone. He had no idea where. I left everything behind, I had not crossed the border into South Africa. He knew that I could not leave without his permission, so he felt smug. Nevertheless, I had vanished. Gone, too, was his child. I do not think he cared too much whether I stayed or not, but my taking his daughter was a big blow. For all his power and connections, he had been outwitted by a mere female. Why I had left in such a hurry was a puzzle, not only to him but also to his family. It was only when my father drove to Durban to pick me up and phoned Armando to tell him that we were safe in Johannesburg in the bosom of the family that my husband knew, for all his threats and bombast, that he had lost the first round.

TOM, TOM, TOM!

I had returned to live with my parents and was working full-time. My grandmother was my safety net. She stayed home and looked after my small baby. This made me feel liberated and was an enormous asset in my very difficult life. I obtained a posting in a very fine girls' school, Auckland Park Girls' Preparatory School, and earned the princely sum of twenty rand a month. This amount was enough to feed a fish, no doubt, but it pained me a great deal that, despite my best efforts and having a degree, I could not support myself, let alone my child. The salaries of women were painfully low. After all, it was possible to hire a black South African for even less for certain jobs, and the South Africans had families to feed, too!

I enrolled in another degree course, this time seeking a master's degree in special education. There were three-hour classes twice a week. Apart from the lectures and coursework, students had to produce a thesis on some aspect of education. School was out for the day at one o'clock, when I rushed up to the university in another part of town. Then, loaded with books and schoolwork to mark for the next day, I took the tram back home. I took over the tending of my baby in order to give my grandmother a break. It was fortunate that my parents had Chico, our cook, to take command of the household and act mainly as chief cook and bottle washer. When my parents arrived from work at about six in the evening, they could relax, eat a well-prepared meal, and unwind after a strenuous day. I recall, too, that we had a younger man who had the strange name of Pencil. He made beds, cleaned house, and went to the store for supplies. Once a week, he filled the bath with soapsuds and did all our laundry by hand. After a while, my father bought a washing machine for Pencil, but it was regarded as an extravagance, as there were many "idle hands" willing to do the job.

It seemed that we, the masters and the servants, all worked very hard. My days were impossibly busy and stressed. I wanted so much to be independent and make my own way, but life seemed stacked against me. In the evenings, I had to study and prepare for the teaching the next day, as well as do work required for the university courses I was taking. I never went out with anyone. Life was hard.

In the midst of a life that bordered on the verge of despair, my life took a glorious turn for the better and changed dramatically.

A school friend from my convent days was a great tennis player and also did a lot of skating at the local rink. I saw very little of her with my tight schedule. Although we sometimes talked on the phone, I never had the time to do some of the exciting things that she had the time to indulge in. One day, she phoned me and asked me to go skating with her at the local rink. We could spend some time together and remind ourselves of the schooldays we had shared.

I hired an extra nanny so my grandmother would not have extra responsibilities, and I went off with guilty feelings to the ice rink, quite a distance from where I resided. I felt like a teenager. At the rink, I had fun doing pirouettes and skating along like a bird. I was feeling liberated. I was, if the truth be known, showing off! I came around the corner at some speed on one leg, failed to negotiate the bend as required, and crashed into the barrier at top speed! It was quite a bang. I should have known better! But within seconds, strong hand picked me up off the ice and dragged me onto a chair. A tall and handsome man had been observing the proceedings while drinking a cup of tea. He patted me down, ordered a cup of tea for me, asked whether I was hurt, and proceeded to chat amicably, as if we had known each other forever.

"You can call me Tom," he said, smiling. I told him my name. "So, you are not a local," he said. I explained that I was Portuguese but that in every other sense I was "local," for I had been born in Johannesburg. "I am a Canadian who is far from home, just as I like it!" he quipped. He ordered another tea and told me that he was coaching the local hockey club, teaching young boys how to play Ice Hockey. He had been given an apartment in the ice rink which, I later learnt, he shared with a hockey friend from England. He was easy to talk to, very unaffected, and interested in everything around him. We talked for over an hour. When I got up to go home, he asked me to come to the rink the following week so I could tell him more about South Africa and its history. I promised him that I would, but I did explain that I had a small child and that my life was not only complicated but also hard.

I recall that I was not able to go to the rink the following week. I found out that my friend Yvette had been questioned as to my whereabouts. She had given Tom my phone number. Tom phoned on the following Friday and asked me to come out to the rink, offering to help me with my skating. I could not do this, as Lena was sick and had to go to the doctor. It was two weeks before I was able to go skating again.

When I went back to the Ice Rink, Tom met me outside and had a special table set up with sandwiches and cake. We talked more than we skated, and it seemed that we had much to talk about. My feeling was that he was a generous, insightful, and caring person with not a skerrig of self-importance. He often put himself down in telling tales about his adventurous life. But he was interested in finding out details of South Africa and accepting ideas about where he should travel in order to get a feel of the land and its people.

He did not talk about himself, although he joked that he was a Londoner, in that his family were Brits who had immigrated to, but left Canada during the Depression days, never to return.

Tom had been travelling the world, trying to see as much of it as possible, as far as his hockey connections would allow. He said he had stayed behind in Canada as a boy on his own, surviving the bleak Depression days by playing hockey, and that he was merely continuing to do this in these better days. He had played on the team that won the World Games in hockey, and he had been a coach to the Swiss Olympic Team. He considered all this a means to an end. He just liked to see the world and found this the most accessible way to do it, especially after his stint as a captain in the Canadian Armed Forces.

I then invited him to come on a Saturday to meet my family. He arrived the following Saturday with flowers for my mother and immediately connected with my small daughter. We had an interesting afternoon, during which my father seemed to enjoy Tom's company. I recall that they discussed politics and the apartheid problems in South Africa.

I continued my harried life, and only occasionally was able to go skating. Tom continued to phone me. He asked me to spend an entire Sunday with him and, this time, bring Lena with me. We went to a park called Zoo Lake, where there was entertainment in the form of families of ducks and two Australian black swans. My daughter was entranced. We sat on the lawn and talked. I learnt a great deal about Tom's life, and he about mine. We had, from the start, an easy relationship. He was, and is, generous of spirit, honest, and sometimes brutally frank, especially about himself. I was enjoying the attention, but mostly I was enjoying the connection of friendship. We discussed all manner of things and life in general, seeming to find common ground at every level. He was shy to ask me about my religious beliefs, as he presumed that I had been brought up Catholic, like my parents and all good Portuguese girls. I disabused him of that notion soon enough and told him how I had been cajoled into a convent education, but that I had long ago decided that, to me, Christianity was but a fairy tale. As such, I would not have any part of it. I had spent much time getting up at 5.00 a.m. to get to Mass, which was obligatory, and then smuggling in books of English poetry to alleviate the tedium of my time in church. I could not wait to get away from Catholicism! Tom was relieved to hear this. Religion held as much interest for me as it had always had for him. None! It is interesting that both of us are rather sedate and very moral individuals, who neither smoke nor drink, and always 'seek to do the right thing' in every situation, between ourselves and in regard to others and we both have very high ethical standards.

It proved difficult for us to see each other, as there were time constraints, work, and family obligations in the way. Tom plotted a way out of these dilemmas. We would plan a Saturday morning meeting and go with a bunch of his friends from the rink to the nearest courthouse and get married! With this in mind, we let my grandmother in on the secret plot. We waited for a long weekend to escape to the countryside to a small town for the ceremony, as all the local magistrate courts were filled weeks in advance. I arranged to take my daughter to the house of my friend Yvette, so that Tom and I would be free to go and do the dreadful deed.

It sounded a simple plan, but it was fraught with problems in the execution. Every courthouse within a reasonable distance from Johannesburg was booked solid, so Tom arranged, with a friend from the rink, to drive us out of town to Vereeniging on the Transvaal–Orange Free State border, where there appeared to be an opening for the marriage ceremony.

I had bought myself a modest dress in a creamy beige with a circular skirt, as was the fashion in those days. Tom went all out and gave me as a wedding present a set of exquisite lingerie: I felt like a queen! The maintenance man at the rink, whom Tom had known in England, loaned us the car and drove us all the way out into the Transvaal countryside. We sang all the way. We giggled at all kinds of idiotic things. When we arrived at the courthouse, we tried to gather our scattered wits before following a couple into the inner sanctum to meet the judge. It looked as if the couple ahead of us had been rolling in the hay. The back of the groom's jacket was laced with bits of straw. Tom made a comic remark about the man's having spent the night rolling in the hay. By the time Tom and I got to the judge, we were hysterical with laughter.

I cannot recall the proceedings, except to say that I was trying to look solemn but barely succeeded. Tom had bought me a ring with two rows of diamonds, and with a row of rubies in between. It was gorgeous! I do not like jewellery normally but I loved to wear my wedding ring!

Tom and I kissed on the courthouse steps after the ceremony and then drove back to Johannesburg, singing and giggling all the way.

Tom was no slouch. He had booked us into the posh Langham Hotel and into their best suite. When we arrived, we got a phone connection in the suite lounge and spent the entire afternoon phoning friends and informing them that we had done the dreadful deed. Would they like to come for a drink with us to celebrate the occasion? There were gasps of incomprehension. I spoke to Tom's friends, and he spoke to mine. "Gosh golly! I never would have expected that from you!" "What, a Canadian?" "What, a Portuguese girl?" Two of Tom's friends worked at the Canadian Consular Services in the embassy. Tom joked that he had invited day and night to visit us that evening. I only caught on when they both arrived breathless, wanting to inspect the bride and introducing themselves as Day and Knight …

I phoned people on my list, all of whom were caught off guard and utterly surprised that Tom had committed the ultimate folly. What a shame! He had been such a steady and responsible fellow. People arrived with their tennis rackets. They were not prepared for this type of news on a quiet Saturday, on a long weekend.

Tom kept phoning the kitchen orders department for more snacks, and these kept arriving, as they had been prepared at short notice. More startled friends came to see what kind of folly was being perpetrated. Tom ordered Champagne. The constant arrival of yet other surprised friends and the ensuing introductions kept the party going. I must admit that I seldom went to parties. I had sometimes relieved my mother of official duties at the consular events, but this party was one of the nicest and friendliest I had ever attended. Later, when it was all over and the last friend departed close to midnight, I phoned to check up on my little daughter who was ensconced at my best friend's house. She had resented being there. She had cried, made a scene, and made my friend feel bad because she couldn't console her. It was only a month later that Tom remarked that he had forgotten to order a wedding cake! I assured him that it had not been missed, that the wedding party was wonderful as it was, and that I would remember it forever!

The next day, Tom phoned my parents and asked them to join us for lunch. They came, with my grandmother in tow, to meet the groom and wish us well. My father, who liked Tom from the start, suggested that, after the honeymoon was over, we should move into his house so that my daughter could remain in the bosom of the family. We decided that we would like to do just that while we cast about for a solution to our living situation. My grandmother was delighted to have us home. Lena settled down to a routine and warmed to Tom's joking and games. I went on working and studying.

My new husband and I found a new house being built a block away and, having looked it over, decided to buy it. We were in a marvellous situation – near the family, but not underfoot. My father often invited us to come over for meals on weekends. He enjoyed Tom a great deal. Even our long-term cook, Chico, was apt to make special Portuguese snacks "just for Tom." So started a lifelong relationship, with all the ups and downs, with the tragedy of losing members of my family, and with our final exodus from Africa.

THE DENTIST

It was a bright, sunny morning and the first day of my first teaching assignment in an elementary school. I had only just started to get to know the other teachers and the children in my grade-three class. I was enthusiastic and eager, but, on this particular day, I was dragging my feet, or, more particularly, dragging my jaws around in agony. It had started with a toothache and progressed to agonizing pain, a swollen face, and increasingly incomprehensible speech. By mid-morning, painkillers had ceased to be effective. My jaw throbbed. The children, sensing my vulnerability, became increasingly rowdy and were pushing the limits of acceptable behaviour.

I gave up, informed the principal of my plight, and fled to the phone booth, where I made two urgent calls. The first was to my friendly dentist, inappropriately named Dr Toews. I got an immediate appointment and was told to make sure to have someone in my family take me home, as, after the procedure, driving was not recommended.

To this end, I left messages with my husband's secretary, informing her of my problems and asking her to make sure that Tom came to the surgery to pick me up after work. Tom was often out in the field. His secretary promised that she would leave him an appropriate urgent message. For good measure, I also phoned my dad, explaining my predicament and the problem of Tom's being away from the office for the day. Would he come to my aid if Tom was unavailable? These were the days before the advent of cell phones. Dad promised to keep his finger on the pulse of things, and I was relieved.

In a blur of pain, I caught a taxi and arrived at Dr Toews's surgery. I was admitted almost right away. Dr Toews then proceeded to extract an offensive impacted wisdom tooth. I remember that I bled a good deal and that I was seated on a chair in a very groggy condition, feeling the worse for wear and trying to recover my bruised dignity.

Dad was in the waiting room. As soon as I was ready to leave, he quickly ushered his swollen-faced daughter into his car and rushed me, dazed and groggy, to his home.

It was well after five o'clock when Tom arrived at the surgery. He had only just received the message: "Pick up your wife at Dr Toews's ASAP. Serious dental procedure – will need ride home," the note read. It was written on pink inter-office memo paper. "URGENT," in large block letters, was heavily underlined.

Tom rushed up a flight of stairs at Dr Toews's and, out of breath, blurted out to the receptionist, "I have come for my wife." The reception area was empty of patients, but Tom was instructed to sit down to wait. The receptionist was busy organizing files when Tom caught the sounds of moaning from the inner sanctum. "What is happening?" he ventured to ask.

"It may take a while," said the receptionist. "You have to understand that it is quite traumatic to have all one's teeth pulled out, but I am sure it was a necessary procedure. She will, no doubt, feel much better once it is all over."

Tom blanched. He felt glued to the seat. "All her teeth?" he enquired.

"I believe so," was the reply. "When the teeth are loose, it is the only option."

The receptionist continued with her work, coming and going with paperwork and files. Tom, stunned, was having difficulty breathing and processing the information.

"She didn't tell me," said Tom weakly. He was beginning to sweat. The sounds from the surgery grew louder.

"I am leaving now," said the receptionist, "but I am sure that your wife will be out shortly." Tom looked at his watch. He was beginning to feel numb as the full realization of the situation dawned on him.

Questions arose in his mind. Why had his wife not confided in him? Why had such a serious problem been kept from him? What else could his wife be keeping from him? Were there to be more horrific secrets uncovered?

Tom got up and paced the floor. More moans could be heard emanating from behind the surgery door.

So young, too, he thought. *How will she go through life with no teeth?* He could not bear the thought of a mouth of false teeth. It gave him the chills.

Finally, after a tortuous half hour, the surgery door opened and out stumbled a dishevelled older woman, still holding a bloodied tissue to her mouth.

Tom stood up and gasped. He rushed up to the unsuspecting patient and declared in a loud voice, "But you are not my wife!"

The astounded woman looked at Tom with incomprehension. "Of course not," she mumbled, thinking Tom demented.

Tom stood rooted to the floor and then, suddenly, gathered himself up and barrelled through the door, went down the stairs, and walked to the parking area. He was very angry. Once in the car, he overshot the speed limit and roared up the driveway to our house. I was not home. Getting angrier by the minute and feeling a mixture of frustration and relief, he then roared up the driveway to my parents' house. He rushed through the door, his mind in a turmoil. There was a great deal he wanted to say. How dare anyone put him through the agony of the last few hours? He found me lying on the sofa, looking swollen and forlorn.

Suddenly, he forgot his anger as he put his arms around me. "Thank goodness you still have all your teeth!" he cried. It was only much, much later that I understood what he meant by that remark.

Last of the River Bushment. Grandmother from the original tribes of Egypt.

Farewell Gathering of the tribes, including Batawana. Herreros from Namibia, and the River Bushmen. Note: Herrero man in foreground is nearly seven feet tall, while River Bushmen are about four feet tall.

Sleeping arrangements. (River Bushmen) Botswana Bedrooms in the Bush, near Maun Botswana.

Batawana women.

Mokorros on the Kwaai.

Mother and child.

Batawana Family.

After a big kill, swollen stomachs. Near Maun, Botswana.

Manuela in Zulu Rickshaw in Durban, Natal. S.A. 1962.

Robyn and Mother, fishing. Durban Rocks

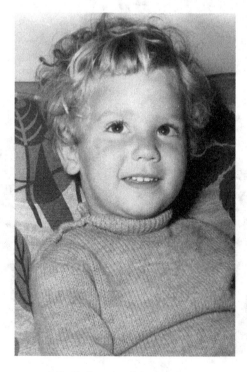

Robyn aged 2 years.

Robyn watching Dad at Hockey.

Rob and friend reading.

Tom and Manuela's first date.

Tom, Captain in Canadian Forces

*June Kaye, Author, and Manuela,
in the Okovongo swamp.*

Mr. and Mrs. Jorge at diplomats ball.

*Manuela's first Graduation from
Witswatersrand University.*

Bicha at 86. In Johannesburg on her Birthday.

Tom and Robyn in Vancouver, Canada in 1985

SATURDAY MORNING AT THE CORNER STORE

It was one of those radiantly bright mornings typical of the winter days on the Highveld of the Witwatersrand. The air felt transparent but very cold, lending a shimmer to all it touched.

My children had awakened early; there was a certain air of expectation for the days when Tom was home. There were always adventures afoot when both parents were home and the day was set aside to cater to the whims of the children. On that particular day, it was decided that we would all take the stroll up the hill to buy some groceries from our Greek shopkeeper, Mr Karadas. We walked hand in hand; Robyn, our son who was then five years old, would have a great time swinging free and holding onto both parents' hands, shrieking with delight.

We arrived at the store entrance almost at the same time as a navy blue police van entered the car park. Two large policemen got out of their transport. One was white; the other, the first's adjutant, was black. They went into the store ahead of us. We saw them talking to Mr Karadas, who told the sad tale of a boy who had entered the store in the night through a transom window and had spent the night eating his way through the fruit and candy in the displays. The police took notes. Then, they went out towards the back of the store, opened a small door, and yanked a tiny, bedraggled, very thin African child of about six or seven years out of the depths of the cupboard. The child was dirty, ragged, and barefooted, and his clothes were merely rags that barely covered his tiny frame. His khaki jacked had only one sleeve, leaving the other arm naked, while part of its front was torn and hanging by a thread. He had the air of extreme emaciation and poverty, shivering as much from the cold as from fright. Terror was etched on his thin face.

The black policeman grabbed the boy roughly and shouted at him in an African language which I could not identify. Then, to my horror, he lifted the boy into the air with one hand and then threw him with force to the ground. We were stunned. We stopped dead in our tracks. My son, Robyn, hid his face in my skirt and would not look at the scene in front of him.

Then we saw a large boot descending on the boy. The white policeman joined his acolyte in kicking the child in the back while he lay helpless on the floor. I can still recall the large black lace-up boots with their thick regulation soles descending on the frail figure of the tiny child. We could hear his bones break when he was kicked. I was so shocked that I became immobilized. Tom, however, retained his cool. He advanced towards the child on the floor and faced the two policemen. I had never seen Tom angry. He is generally peaceful and conciliatory, but, on this occasion, he was fierce. The police tried to move towards him, but Tom held his ground. The small boy was still whimpering.

I had sudden visions of Tom's being taken away for interfering in police business. I came and stood in front of him. Robyn came with me, his head still engulfed in my skirt, pretending that he had not seen the violence perpetrated on the small boy. Lena was rooted to the ground. She did not move. She seemed not to comprehend what was happening. Her face was impassive with disbelief.

I clung onto Tom. I knew that he was at the point where only a very little would put him over the edge. I could only imagine the consequences if he tackled two policemen. I clung to his arm. The white policeman seemed to understand that the public display of brutality was not going down well, so he went around Tom and me, roughly picked up the bleeding boy, and threw him into the back of the police van with a thud. The child was covered in blood. Then, the two policemen got into the van and went off, leaving behind a cloud of dust and gravel.

Mr Karadas was straightening the merchandise that the small intruder had disturbed and went on as if this was just another insignificant episode in his daily life. We did not buy what we had come to the store to purchase. Instead, we left silently, Robyn still clinging to my skirt, Tom hanging onto my hand on one side and Lena's on the other. We said nothing. What could have been said in the face of these brutal events? All the way home, there was a deathly silence as if we were all trying to sort out reactions to events that did not make sense.

We never spoke of the incident. But come Monday morning, Tom asked me whether it was time to put our house up for sale. I agreed instantly. The die was cast. We could not, in all conscience, go on living and planning a future in this country. Tom and I had, for a long period time, been witness to events that we could barely understand. We decided to take a stand. We could not stay in a country with so much violence perpetrated daily on the black population.

Within three months, we had got rid of most of our belongings, sold the house, and subsequently moved into the university residence for graduates of the University of the Witwatersrand at Frankenwald. We were waiting for me to complete my graduate thesis.

Then, suddenly, my grandmother fell in the bath and subsequently died of her injuries. Then, just as suddenly, my dad became ill and was in and out of hospital over a period of months. Tom, I, and our children had been due to sail for Australia from Durban and had booked our passage. We cancelled it. We could not leave knowing how ill my father was.

Life dragged on. All around us was the discord caused by apartheid, the continued brutality of the Afrikaner regime that had come to power, ubiquitous pass laws, the creation of the Bantustans, the loss of habeas corpus, and the imprisonment of white dissenters under ninety-day arrest laws. Things were indeed going from bad to worse – "To hell in a hand basket," as Tom put it.

DURBAN, NATAL, DELIGHT!

Tom had been asked to go down to Durban, which, after the climate of Johannesburg, was sheer heaven. How did we get so lucky? The climate of Johannesburg is, by South African standards, just awful. The Whitewaters Ridge ("Witwatersrand") is seven thousand feet up on the largest ridge of gold in the world. Mostly, people think of Africa as a hot and steamy place with a benign climate. Nothing could be further from the truth when describing the Transvaal I winter. Going to Durban seemed like a reprieve.

Living on the Whitewaters Ridge was hateful for several reasons. The winters were not enhanced by white snow but by dry, freezing winds engulfing the city in the yellow dust that penetrated every crevice and dried out any uncovered skin. It never, ever rained in winter. We had to wait for the summer for the rain to appear somewhat apologetically. Every afternoon, like clockwork, it would shower. It would last about half an hour, and then the clouds would disappear, almost apologetically, and everyone would go about their business as if nothing had happened. It was almost useless to carry an umbrella. I certainly never had one. But winter was nonetheless harsh. I went to school and had a chapped face. Schools were not centrally heated, so, as children, we sat on the water-filled heaters and got burnt bottoms.

Flying into the city, one is able to see one of the ugliest scenes in all the Transvaal. Large mounds of golden-coloured dust piles form artificial "mountains" around the city and speak of the ground removed from below the buildings. When I was a child, there were always blasts during the day. These would shake the buildings just like earthquakes do. Nobody seemed to care about the wobbles. My mother would go up to a picture swinging on the wall, steady it, and not even miss a sentence of conversation.

Transvaal's population is the most diverse. The white population consisted of the Afrikaners (Dutch) and the English who had taken the territory from the embattled Boers after the Boer War. A large assortment of Europeans had immigrated to try their luck in a "new" country. Then there were the indigenous people of various races, clans, and tribes (thirty-two from within South Africa alone, all with distinct cultures, histories, and languages). Added to the mix were the black tribesmen who, each year, immigrated to the Transvaal to try their luck in the mines. They arrived without families, lived in male hostels, and often whiled away their free time by drinking intoxicating drinks in *shebeens* (illicit beer parlours). Walking down the street, one could sense a certain European elegance and sophistication. But on the same sidewalk, there would be bare-breasted, barefooted black women walking with babies on their backs and wearing beaded skirts and headdresses. Johannesburg is a city of skyscrapers. At one time, there were more in Jo'burg than in New York City. It is a city of great schools, world-famous universities, and a high crime rate. The institutions of the mining school were without equal. They were then, as now, held in worldwide regard. People seemed to be in Johannesburg to get on with their jobs in a serious frame of mind. University students were not a frivolous and fun-loving group. They were a serious-minded cache of earnest young adults who spent most of their time with their noses in books.

A large plaque had been erected in the main foyer of the University of the Witwatersrand, dedicated to the acceptance of everyone, without regard to creed or race, into its fold. When I attended the university, the plaque had been forcibly removed by the apartheid government. My best friend, who happened to be an Indian from Goa, was asked to leave, despite great grades, because she was "of colour"!

I joined the black-sash movement. It consisted of a group of well-educated women who wore black sashes over their dresses to "mourn the death of the Constitution and the removal of the habeas corpus clause from the South African Constitution." This meant that there needed not be probable cause to arrest someone. It could be done with impunity and on the whim of the government or the police.

My father did not approve of my affiliations. We were foreigners, he said, who had to be impartial in this country that was not our own. To me, who had never been to Europe, this was the only country I had known, and I felt strongly about the injustices being perpetrated by the government.

I recall spending long hours before finals with my Indian friend Amina. It was two in the morning when we finally went to bed. Tom took Amina home at that late hour and was accosted by the police. Where was he going at the late hour? Did he not know that it was illegal for a white man to consort with an Indian? Tom was livid and explained that he was not "consorting" but was, in fact, taking Amina home. The police held him and phoned me to establish the veracity of the story before they released him!

The great university celebration was called Rag Day. There was a parade with floats made by the students. Everyone wore fancy costumes. I was co-opted to go on the mining engineers' float. We had a royal time. It was the only occasion where I recall that the priority lay elsewhere, not in the proverbial book! It was years later when I verified the immense quality of the education I had received at Witwatersrand, for which I am eternally grateful.

*   *   *

We had been given a reprieve of sorts. Tom was being moved to Durban!! This was a city that was in the tropics, on the ocean, and filled with holiday tourists escaping Johannesburg. I was ecstatic! This was like getting out of a life sentence. We went down with high expectations. I had not completed my thesis, but I was prepared to do it the hard way – from a distance!

I left in my small Mini-Minor with a profusion of luggage, two crying children, neither of whom was taking kindly to the idea of leaving the bosom of the family, and a beloved great-grandmother. The children waved goodbye, promptly burst into tears, and were inconsolable. The trip in the car was a nightmare! I put a brave front on things and talked about the ocean, the beaches, and how nice it would feel to be in the warm climate and on the sands with the waves coming into shore to meet us. After a while, the children curled up in each other's arms and fell into the sleep of the emotionally exhausted. Tom had gone ahead to start work and make arrangements for an apartment for our family.

The journey was not a long one. It was about three hundred miles to the coast, and I had expected it to take all day. The children were feeling sorry for themselves. I, exceptionally tired, made several stops to break the solitude and distract them from their misery. When we finally pulled into Durban, it was a great relief. We all felt that we had accomplished a feat of endurance. We found the proverbial light at the end of the tunnel. I had the address of the apartment that Tom had rented for us. At about five that evening, we arrived, weary, at the apartment building. I was not feeling well; in fact, I had developed a severe migraine and was feeling quite nauseous. There was nowhere to sit, as the furniture had not yet arrived, so I took myself off to the toilet and sat on the seat, looking utterly exhausted after the long drive. Robyn started to cry, having expected Tom to be there waiting for us. I joined him, not for the same reason, but because I was ill, completely exhausted, and feeling sorry for myself! The building superintendent came to see how we were getting on, knowing that our furniture had not yet arrived, and found me crying with Robyn on my lap, crying in sympathy. I assured the superintendent that our things would be arriving shortly, that Tom would arrive momentarily, and that all would be well.

We waited and waited. I continued sitting on the toilet seat with Robyn on my lap. Tom had still not arrived, and our possessions had not been delivered. The super looked in on me and finally decided, on his own, to call on a doctor who lived in the building to provide some assistance. The doctor arrived, tended to me (still sitting on the toilet seat), and gave me an injection that knocked me out. I curled up in a ball. When Tom arrived, I was curled up on the bathroom floor with Robyn in my arms, completely out of it! Tom negotiated with the movers to install the beds as a first priority. He put me to bed in the bedroom, closed the door, and then took the children out to eat, while the movers proceeded to bring out things from the truck and pile them on the living room floor in complete disarray.

So started our new life in Durban, the city of my dreams! Things could only look up from there! They could only get better and better – which they eventually did!

SUNSHINE AND TREE MAMBAS

Tom and I looked for accommodation in Durban and found it in Umgeni Heights. The area was situated on top of a mountain which afforded views of the distant sea. We could not afford a new house, so we settled for an older one which needed upgrading but had oodles of space and a garden area in front about one acre in size. As the houses in front of us were situated at the bottom of the rise, our view could never be built out. The rooms in the house were all huge, and our furniture looked rather ridiculous in these cavernous spaces. The problem was that, while the bedrooms were huge, we had only two of them. The result was that when my grandmother decided to come down to live with us, which overjoyed me, she had to share the enormous space with the children. Our living room was fifty feet long and emptied into a cavernous dining room that looked forlorn with only the table and chairs. As the old houses had, our house had a red-polished veranda looking out over our large garden and the distant sea.

There were some fruit trees in the garden as well as a garage that had seen better days; it tilted slightly before Tom propped it up. We desperately needed a gardener to mow the huge lawn and tidy the trees. We hired an elderly Indian man with impeccable manners and let him loose on the weeds and the huge front lawn. In the first week, I noticed that there seemed to be something green going along the front lawn (from left to right) and disappearing into a large fruit tree. I thought that my eyes were playing tricks on me and dismissed the vision as an illusion. A week later, the same thing happened. When I investigated, I found nothing. I sent the gardener to investigate. He reported that he saw nothing unusual. The neighbour's children came over to play with our children and had a royal time running hither and thither. One afternoon, while sitting on the veranda, I saw a green flash. Now I knew that I had not been dreaming! Our gardener investigated and found that there was a huge green mamba snake making a beeline for the fruit tree every afternoon at about two o'clock. He did not seem alarmed and assured me that the animal followed a pattern. It slept in one area and then looped and slithered across the lawn after lunch to sleep in the tree. It was not perturbed. I gave the children strict instructions to stay out of the tree and *not* ever think of going to play hide-and-seek at the bottom of the garden.

All houses in South Africa had separate "houses" at the back with showers and toilets for the house staff. I promptly hired a nanny, who came to work with a small baby wrapped on her back.

The nanny's baby especially liked to be carried on her mother's back when the mother was ironing. The constant motion put the baby to sleep. One afternoon, I came home from school and found Robyn fast asleep on the nanny's back! I had not anticipated this at all, as Rob was over three years old at the time! I discouraged him and promised to take him and Lena to make cookies in the kitchen if he refrained from sleeping on his nanny's back. It worked like a charm. I had discovered the mother lode. Robyn liked nothing better than to cook, and baking cookies with Mum in the kitchen was at the top of his wish list. (To this day, Rob still likes to cook.)

I took a job in an alternative school. Schools were graded by skin colour in those apartheid days. There were schools for white children, some (but few) schools for black children in the so-called townships, and then the ubiquitous schools for those in between. These children were often of so-called white parentage. They had turned out to be a little too dark to be considered "lily white," and so the government, in its wisdom, decided, to put these children into a separate school. Often, one child in the family was segregated from his or her siblings. As can be imagined, these separated children were often rebellious and maladjusted, due entirely to their misguided segregation, I suspect, and nothing else.

As the boys in my class tested me and tried to write rude and suggestive words on the blackboard, I ignored them and then decided that the best policy was to tackle issues head-on. I confronted the class and asked them whether they would really like to know about some of the subjects they had written on the blackboard. They were aghast that I would tackle such taboo subjects. But I did, in a matter-of-fact and scientific way. When I did, you could hear a pin drop in my normally rowdy class.

I taught science and math and enjoyed the children a great deal. They knew that they could not humiliate me and that I was willing to tackle any subject head-on. As a matter of course, I was assigned to playground duty one day every week. I would see to it that the younger children played without hurting themselves. On one particular day, a small boy of about eight or nine fell out of a tree when the branch broke. He was thrown to the ground, falling on his wrist. It was quite a severe break, and so I took him back into the school building and was informed by the staff that the best thing would be to take him to hospital almost immediately. We wrapped his broken wrist in a small towel, and I popped the boy on the back seat and drove him as quickly as possible to the nearest hospital. When we arrived at the inpatient section, I was told that that they would not take the boy. I was stunned! "Is this not a hospital?" I enquired. "Why can you not help?" At first, I realize now, it was thought that I was the child's mother, and so I was given knowing looks of disapproval! I was then shown the door, indicating, in no uncertain terms, that I should leave. I had no idea where a "coloured" hospital might be, so I asked for directions.

Finally, I arrived at another clinic. They treated the boy right away and kept looking at me to explain my relationship to him. I got on the phone, called his mother, explained where I was, and asked her to meet me. She arrived in short order. I was most surprised when, instead of being glad that the boy had been given medical attention, she said rudely, "Get him out of here, I do not want him to go to a black hospital! You should have notified me! I know where to take him! You don't!" She pushed the boy out the door and left me standing in the lobby!

*   *   *

The school year in South Africa ends in December (unlike in North America). Tom had been taking photographs in the Port of Durban. He and Robby wanted to sneak off to "see the big ships." For a change, I decided to go with them. I made some sandwiches and a flask of tea, and off we went. Then, Tom made an interesting remark. "It is about time that you went to see some of the world," he said. "You have not seen anything yet! I have been all over the place. It should be your turn now!" I did not take it seriously and, in view of my responsibilities and lack of money, thought it a bit of a joke. But Tom was deadly serious.

"I have been thinking that while we are in Durban, in the big house, and Bicha is living with us, you should go, take a year off, and see Europe, at least. The children will be fine. I will keep an eye on things, and you can have a good time for a change!" said Tom.

"What will I do for money?" I asked

"I have the *big plan* in place," Tom replied. He had obviously been thinking about it for a while. Then and there, he laid it all out! I would sell my small car and use the money to keep me on my travels. Tom would "lend" me money to buy a Volkswagen Kombi from Germany and have it delivered to Naples in Italy. In this I could live and travel around the European continent. When I returned, I would sell the vehicle and pay only the depreciation. If I could "share" the car with another woman, then the travels would be quite inexpensive. As a first step in the right direction, Tom, the children, and I could all get on a ship and go as far as Zanzibar, and then I would go on through Suez to Italy. There, I would pick up the Volkswagen, proceed to see some of the continent, and meet my Portuguese family in Lisbon and Tom's family in London.

By the time we got back for dinner, the nefarious plans were laid. I was terribly excited and asked Bicha to stay on at the house and keep an eye on things (Robyn in particular). Bicha was very glad for me and said that I had struggled enough and was finally getting my just reward. She was happy to see me being rewarded for a change. I could not believe my good fortune!

I was on cloud nine! It would be so wonderful to have the family with me for the start of my great adventure!

So it was that the plans were made. Later, we went down to the docks to catch the ship to Europe. My "schoolboys" all came down to the docks and aboard the ship to see me off and give me hugs of goodbye. They brought me a huge bunch of South African Proteas along with their good wishes for a wonderful trip. I was very happy! How lucky could one young woman get?

* * *

As it turned out, I did exactly as planned and saw a great deal of Europe (as well as Scandinavia). I had posted a request in Canada House in London for a travelling companion, and one materialized in the form of a lovely woman from Montreal. She joined me in my travels, and we shared the expenses. I recall that I spent a total of seven dollars a day, including gasoline and food! Those were the days, and they make for a separate story!

I had gone to Lisbon towards the end of my travels and had met my Portuguese family. They were old-fashioned, staid, and somewhat stuffy, regarding me as an extraterrestrial.

I had gone through various countries in Europe and found the experience interesting, but nowhere did I find the culture shock that I experienced in Lisbon with my large Portuguese family. They were kindly, curious, and filled with wonder at this strange woman who strutted around in *pants!* Nobody in their right mind wore those, especially not to the city! Perhaps they were appropriate on a beach, but in the centre of Lisbon, hardly! I did not want to offend, but there were limits to what I could or would do. I was immediately told that a minor uncle would be liberated in order to accompany me. When I asked what for, my relatives said that a married woman should not go alone into the city. I shrieked with laughter and told them that I had travelled unescorted all over Europe and Scandinavia and that it was ludicrous for me to be accompanied in broad daylight now that I was in a country where I knew my way around and whose language I spoke fluently.

I was invited to huge meals, not only in terms of the dishes offered, but also in terms of the family members who joined me to "examine" the strange relative from Africa. Lunch would take three hours. Dish after dish arrived, and I found it impossible to cope with the variety and quantity offered. I finally found a way out! I let it be known that I adored shellfish. Thereafter at lunch, I had a plate of delicious small clams that took a great deal of time to disengage from the shells. Once eaten, after considerable effort, they left a tell-tale mound of small shells that bespoke of a huge meal when, in fact, they were "slim pickings." I could extend the eating of clams for an indefinite period. In between the lengthy conversations, it was not noticed that I really ate very little.

I noticed that houses in Portugal had very small living rooms. These were only to admit strangers, whereas family and friends were always led into the dining room. These were huge and always had many extra seats, even if the family living in the house consisted of only four people.

I had the feeling that I had been transported into the Middle Ages. It was only when I met cousins, one a lawyer, and another with a doctorate in Greek and Latin, that I began to shine a little. My relatives' attitudes changed when I started to have "intelligent conversations."

I managed to worm my way into the affections of the family and, in the weeks I stayed in Portugal, make some genuine friendships. But at no time did I feel any affiliation to the culture, except superficially. Despite having been educated in that far distant and dark continent of Africa, I knew in my bones that I was far ahead in my thinking and that I could never live in the stifling environment that was a male-dominated and church-ridden Portuguese society of the time.

AN INCIDENT AT FRANKENWALD

A patchwork of dark brown earth alternating with black scorched grasses paint sombre colours over the shallow rolling hills of the Transvaal veld, bringing winter to undulating hills. The only trees in the stark landscape were giant eucalyptus, which were planted to border the roadway into Frankenwald Experimental Farm. Small bushes, indigenous to the high veld, had long since disappeared to be used as firewood, heating skimpy huts and shacks in the bitter cold of the dry Johannesburg nights.

Half a mile from the road, set back and surrounded by small fields, each fenced off and segregated by barbed wire, lay the experimental fields of the university's botany department. Further on, a cluster of low brick buildings with a larger and more prominently placed mess hall and kitchen building was on an elevated mound surrounded by a small garden. This building had a large veranda of red concrete which shone in the light and attested to the staff members' daily care and polishing.

The community had grown out of housing which was initially intended for married students, mostly returned soldiers displaced by the war who were attempting to pick up where they had left off in their studies before they had been shipped out to fight against Rommel in the deserts of North Africa. All were completing higher degrees. They mostly had children. The red brick bungalows that littered the grounds were their small apartments.

At that period in our lives, Tom and I had already made the decision to leave South Africa and had sold our house. It seemed fortuitous when we found university accommodations at Frankenwald. I qualified for housing there because I was a graduate of the university and was now engaged in a master's-level programme. Living in the students' quarters was an opportunity to live in the country, outside of the Johannesburg city limits and out of the crime-ridden city. There was plenty of room for our family to roam the spacious grounds. We were fortunate to have both a swimming pool and a tennis court at our disposal. I did not have to worry about meals, as they were provided in a common mess hall.

We were transformed from an unsettled family ready to emigrate, to one who enjoyed our environment, the safety it provided, and the space it allowed for the children to play and roam. The intellectual stimulation of being with other families all of whom were equally unsettled and aiming to complete studies so as to move on to fresh pastures, gave us a common purpose.

Meals taken in the mess hall were organized by the Mess Committee. I eventually graduated to chief cook and bottle washer, and chairwoman of the food committee. I loved to cook and bake, so, whenever possible, I planned adventurous forays into foreign cuisine. On Saturdays and Sundays, I produced elaborate cakes which we ate under the large oak tree at the back of the mess hall. Here, we all gathered and had refreshments and lively conversation.

Meal gatherings were a treat. We changed tables at every meal, and, as we were all university graduates, our conversations were informative and lively. There were representatives of many faculties and many differing points of view. Whatever opinion was voiced, there were invariable those with an opposing idea. Discussions could get lively.

I thrived. I can honestly say that this was the most interesting and most intellectually stimulating place in which I have ever lived.

In the political hothouse that South Africa had become, there was no time to examine inconsequential issues. Most discussions were well-informed and heartfelt.

Attached to the mess were two kombi buses, and it was in these that the children were gathered up each morning and then delivered to the local elementary school three miles away.

Robyn loved Frankenwald almost instantly. Instead of being a solitary small boy with busy parents, he suddenly found himself in the centre of rough-and-tumble football games with a motley collection of children, both white and black. He would go hell for leather all afternoon in the rough games and then fall asleep, utterly contented and thoroughly exhausted, each evening. As soon as he arrived from school, our nanny made sure that he changed out of his school uniform and had something to eat before he was allowed to get into the fray and the rough-and-tumble with the other boys. Sometimes, the nanny did not intervene in time and Rob would cast his good Clark's school shoes into a bush in order to get into the fray of the game as soon as he arrived home. He felt that there was not a minute to waste. In three months, he managed to lose five pairs of shoes. Needless to say, after the fifth pair had gone the way of all the others, Tom, scowling with disapproval, threatened Robyn with hidings and severe punishments. We all secretly knew that his growls were worse than his bite and that he would never follow up on his threats.

My daughter did not take to our new environment. She was ashamed that we should live in shabby surroundings and said that our accommodation was little better than the black townships. She went to a "posh" private school, and her classmates had beautiful homes. Lena felt deprived. She always felt that her surroundings reflected on her personally, and she was generally upset by not being one of "the chosen." She complained that I did not attend the mothers' meetings and that I did not help with the making of sandwiches, in which the other mothers were involved. I tried to reason with her and told her that I would contribute in some other way, but that as my life was so busy and my time so restricted, I could not do what the other mothers did. One day, the occasion arose in which I was asked to talk at the parents' meeting about developmental problems in young children. The hall was packed with parents, and the school gave me an enthusiastic introduction. I spoke for an hour and held everyone in rapt attention. After the question period, the mother of one of Lena's classmates remarked that she had not known that Lena had such a remarkable mother. The next day, Lena told me that perhaps I was not as awful as she had thought!

This was also the time when my family had the least amount of material comforts. We certainly had little money. Our apartment was small, and our possessions could have been packed into a few suitcases. The apartment had an oversized living area, a smaller bedroom, and a large storage and bathroom area, but toilets were housed in a separate building. I recall sitting in the toilet with the door opening onto a field where there were always the ubiquitous cows munching their pasture and looking at me languidly through the barbed wire fence.

In winter, the sunshine, harsh and metallic, hardly warms the thin, dry air of the Witwatersrand, which sits at an altitude of seven thousand feet. There are no rains in winter, so that even if the temperature drops well below zero, there is never any snow. The air is so deprived of moisture that children's cheeks are rosy and chapped; often, their lips are cracked. In the hot and languorous summer, however, the rain comes daily and torrentially, but it does not last and often is over within twenty minutes. Umbrellas are out of favour; after all, one has only to wait a short while till the sun reappears from behind fleeting clouds, as if it had been a mistake to hide behind clouds in the first place.

The African staff at Frankenwald lived in small thatched rondavels situated across a small stream, their separation from the white community being required by law. There were thirty or so black farm families. The men were employed working in the fields and helping with the research experiments that were being conducted by the Botany Field Research Department. The women looked after their own small children, but usually also supplemented the family income by obtaining employment aiding the white residents with their domestic arrangements.

I had returned home early from my teaching post at Auckland Park Elementary School. It was midweek and bitterly cold. I had sauntered out to grab a cup of tea under the oak tree, where it was usually set out in the afternoons, to find nothing laid out and no one around. It appeared that the place was deserted. There were no African workers or gardeners in sight. The usual rowdy children were nowhere to be seen. I noted that the kombi bus with the returning children had not yet arrived.

I was surprised but not alarmed. After all it was just an ordinary day in an ordinary week filled with mundane happenings.

Nothing in that cloudless, sunny, chilly winter afternoon could have prepared me for the events that followed – events that still linger like cobwebs in the recesses of my memory, even now after so many years.

* * *

92

Julian was our cook who operated an efficient kitchen and saw to all the meals. He was a fairly well-educated Zulu from the province of Natal. His family was from the region of the Valley with a Thousand Hills. He was highly intelligent and always eager to learn. I had already formed a good relationship with Julian when I offered to "manage" the kitchen. He was delighted when I taught him how to cook Chinese food in a wok. Julian organized the deliveries of vegetables, produce, milk, cream, and eggs from nearby farms and stored them in the large walk-in freezer–refrigerator. I had taught him to make creamed soups as well as an array of cakes and desserts. He had several kitchen helpers who looked after the dining hall, washed the dishes, and kept the kitchen spic and span. Julian was married to a beautiful Xhosa girl with large liquid brown eyes and an easy disposition. Her name was Ula. Tom joked that she could easily be U-la-la.

Ula worked as my nanny. She looked after the children when they came from school on days when I had lectures at the university. Mainly, she kept an eye on Robyn and rescued him from dubious activities, such as attempting to go swimming in the stream that ran behind our residence.

That fateful afternoon, I looked for Ula. She was nowhere in sight.

Three thirty came and went, and I was beginning to feel spooked.

Julian was nowhere to be found; neither were any of his cohorts. I looked around for our gardener, John. He was tall and muscular and had a wonderfully broad and sensitive face. He longed to get an education and, in the evenings, would come back to the kitchen with Shakespearean plays and ask for help in deciphering the language, laughing uproariously at the absurdity of the plots. Many of my colleagues would humour him and teach him "regla and fancy Hinglish" despite the fact that, at the time and under the restrictions recently promulgated by the racist government, it was strictly illegal for a white person to teach an African anything. Doing this could get you jail time.

There was nobody about. I walked around the mess hall and the front and back gardens, but everything was as silent as the tomb.

I was beginning to get alarmed. Then I noticed that someone had entered the kitchen. The large water kettle hissed steam and filled the kitchen with bubbling noises. I hardly recognized Julian when he came in and sat down on his usual stool.

He was dressed as a Zulu warrior. Gone were the sweatshirt and white pants he usually wore as our cook. He was now bare to the waist and wore leggings of hides and feathers, plus a complicated headdress. In his right hand, he carried a knobkerrie. A row of crocodile teeth encircled his neck. He looked straight ahead and ignored me when I tried to talk to him. His demeanour was one of defiance. I attempted to mollify him and kept asking – after saying, "Julian you look very elegant" – "Julian, where is everyone?"

He looked away. He was very angry.

The fact that there was nobody around at a time normally buzzing with activity still puzzled me. I was determined to keep asking until I got a reply. It was obvious to me now that something had gone drastically wrong. As I became more alarmed, I also became more determined to find out what it was.

"Julian, please, please, tell me what has happened," I begged.

Finally, in order to silence me, he replied, "All gone!" He still refused to look at me.

"Who has gone, and where have they gone to?" I persisted.

Julian remained silent. He moved close to the bubbling kettle and did not respond. His anger was palpable.

I continued to ask questions. Finally, in a gesture of annoyance, Julian shouted, "They come and take everyone away! They are all gone!"

"Who came to take everyone away?"

Julian emitted a growl. "The police!" he said with clenched teeth.

"Why would they come here? What did they want?"

"They come in big vans and they take all!"

"Did they say why they did that?"

"They say no signature on all passes," he shouted, "so, they came to take all. They go across the river to every kraal and take all the big people into the vans … they go off quickly, quickly," he said with a look of disgust.

"Do you mean that they came and just took everyone in their vans because of a problem with the passes?"

He nodded, all the while not taking his eyes off the bubbling kettle on the stove, which, at this point, was making protesting noises if its own.

Julian's hands on his knobkerrie were clasped with such force that his knuckles appeared white on his black skin.

Then came a bigger bombshell. "They take all the women right away and won't let them take the piccaninnies."

I could not believe my ears. "So, all the children are left at home with all the babies by themselves – alone?"

Julian nodded. He was not going to add to the conversation. At that moment, the kombis arrived with all the white schoolchildren. I could hear the general melee from the kitchen.

I rushed out and told the children to go home quickly and change into their casual clothes. I explained that we had a problem and that today there was not only no tea, but also were no nannies. There was no playtime, either. I needed their help, I said.

I grabbed Julian by the arm and, with one thought in mind, told him that we had to gather the kombi drivers. We had to go across the river to each kraal and fetch the children and babies who had been left abandoned by the police action. Everyone looked stunned, but they cooperated. The older children were instructed to look after one small baby each, and off we went at great speed over the rutted track to the small rondavels.

As we approached, I could hear babies crying and see distracted small children half dressed in the bitter cold wind, trying to silence their younger siblings, who were crying pitifully in distress.

In the first kraal, we found a tiny baby, a toddler, and a four-year-old trying to pacify his siblings. We picked them up, gathered them in any blankets we could find, and delivered them to the older girls in the van, who immediately assumed the responsibility of looking after their much distressed charges. We went from one kraal to the next and collected eleven newborn babies and twenty-three small children. The kombis were packed like sardines. There was much screaming and wailing while the teenagers tried to assure their charges that all would be well. We disgorged all the children into the warm kitchen and lined them up against the walls like small parcels. Our young white girls cuddled them.

More of our residents had arrived by this time and were apprised of our problems. Everyone pitched in to help. The kitchen was full of bodies doing various chores and coming to the assistance of those in need. Milk bottles appeared, and the small children were given formula or milk. Three women decided to make a large pot of vegetable soup. Soon, mounds of cut-up vegetables were being piled into the steaming pots on the stove.

When one of the men on the faculty arrived, we quickly arranged for him to phone the police station and find out what charges were pending against our staff. This proved complicated. Due to the large numbers of arrests the fact that there were men as well as women in the group, our staff had been sent further afield into a larger holding facility. Nobody could tell us where they were or even what alleged crime had been committed.

Night was falling. More residents arrived on the scene. When told of the state of affairs, everyone tried to help. It was an atmosphere of chaos. Not everyone had a private phone in his or her apartment, but the few who did immediately volunteered to find out as much information as possible from the authorities.

Finally, the pertinent details were assembled; the arrests were made because the farm manager had not signed the passes in a timely fashion. As the date had lapsed, there was now a large fine assessed, which had to be paid first, if we wanted to secure the release of our staff.

No one could come up with the required sum. We were all relatively poor and in the same boat. We had reached an impasse. Where were we to find a large sum of cash at this time of night?

Then a thought occurred to me. I would find Tom at work and tell him of our predicament. He worked for a large ice cream and candy firm in the city. I asked him to beg, borrow, or steal cash in order to get our staff out of prison. I informed him of all the details, as far as I could tell, and he was appalled; but despite the late hour, he promised to come home with the cash. He had a plan in mind. He jumped into his car and proceeded to visit all the cafes and restaurants to which Neilson (based in Canada) supplied food products. He wrote endless Neilson cheques to these firms in exchange for all the cash they might have on hand.

The amount was in excess of a thousand rand, which, in those days, was a fairly large amount of money to carry around as loose change. Tom found us all partaking of the hot soup in the kitchen. Most of the children had been fed and watered, and the smaller ones were sleeping and quiet, when Tom arrived with his bag of money. Five of my colleagues immediately piled into the kombi and went off to the jail to attempt to pay the fine and get our people home. But it was too late in the day. There was nobody around to undertake the paperwork. "Come back tomorrow after nine o'clock," the jail personnel instructed the anxious men. There was nothing to do but drive home, thoroughly dejected. Plans were made to be at the court first thing in the morning in order to retrieve our innocent staff.

Once again, five of the men went to the court, reluctantly accepted the guilty charge, and paid the fine with all the loose change. They protested that the fault lay with the farm manager, who was away; the staff was innocent of any criminal activity.

"So, all these innocent people were arrested when it was the fault of the farm manager?" the men asked. The question was ignored. If you were black in apartheid South Africa, you had no human rights, anyway.

The judge, realizing that there was opposition to such an unfair law, stopped the proceedings and changed the official language to Afrikaans, knowing that at least four of the men present would have no inkling of what was being said. So, it was that without proper representation – and, in fact, not really understanding what offence the staff were purported to have committed – that the fines were paid and the staff released.

Kombis as well several other cars had been driven to the jail. As soon as the formalities were completed, the staff were packed into the vehicles and brought home into the warm kitchen, where their children were returned to them. In addition, we sent each person home with large containers of soup – and a huge milk container for everyone to share. They did not talk much, just picked up their children and began to walk home in relative silence.

It was a Saturday and the beginning of the weekend, but we had all had a ragged day. Many of our residents hung around and tried helping any way they could, still unsettled by the events of the previous evening.

This is what this land had come to. This was why we had three of our residents under house arrest. This was why many had decided to leave. This is why my family lived in Frankenwald and made plans for different lives in other places. We were all outnumbered, outgunned, and outmanoeuvred. There was no justice to be had in this harsh land of unfair pass laws and of no regard given when separating innocent babies from their mothers.

There was much conversation and milling about. More plates of soup were passed around. The women all volunteered to help with the cooking and the feeding of our children, and the dishwashing and chores, usually done by the kitchen staff.

A delegation was organized to go the following Monday to discuss our problems with the manager and to inform the chancellor of the university and the head of the botany department of our predicament. One thing was clear: the farm manager had to go.

We all went to bed tired, but thinking that at least we had done all we could despite circumstances being mostly out of our control. We had tried to help our staff and their families to the best of our ability. I fell asleep almost immediately when I hit the pillow – the sleep of the emotionally exhausted.

Then the fire alarm sounded, and it did not stop. It went on wailing while everyone leapt up in various states of disarray and rushed out into the freezing night. Our fields had all been set alight. Someone had torched them, and the flames attacked the dry veld with a vengeance. We knew that we had to save our residences and our possessions as best we could. We knew, too, that out here, there was no handy fire brigade to call. We were "rural" and, as such, were responsible for our own firefighting.

The men quickly organized themselves into a force. Wet sacks had been commandeered, passed up the line, and beaten vigorously against the burning grasses. The barbed wire was cut down, and there was a lot of slapping and beating of the bushes. The women saw to it that the bags were returned and wet down in large vats, and others carried them to the fields where the harassed men were not making much headway with the flames. Most of them looked like ghosts, black with soot and sweat.

Across the same river that divided the black and the white residents, there was no smoke; there was no fire. All was deathly silent. No one came to our aid. When some of the fires were extinguished in one section, others were started in other fields. We knew that out homes and our lives were in jeopardy. The irony was that we were being punished because we were white. The fact that we protested vigorously to what had happened to our staff, that we had our own people in jail for liberal causes, that we opposed the government at every step … it was just not enough.

It would never be enough to repair the damage caused by the apartheid laws. We were the whites, the ones in power, the ones who were deemed complicit in making the laws. The fact that the Frankenwald residents were intensely against what was happening, was so much water under the bridge.

Tom arrived home black with soot. I organized some towels and soap and a change of clothes, and off he went into the men's showers to clean his body after six hours of firefighting. The fires had been extinguished at long last, the men having come home exhausted but happy that our homes had been saved.

The women continued to organize the food and run the kitchen. We were somewhat disorganized, but at least there was food on the table.

Tom had gone into work and come home with three large insulated containers full of "dented" ice cream packages. These would have been washed down the drains at the factory, but Tom fought with the management, asking them not to waste this resource in a land of so much need.

He arrived triumphant and, together with Robyn, went over to the kraals and called the children so as to give them the goodies. He was mobbed. Once word got out, children from farms over the hills came out to claim the delicious sweets that previously they only dreamed about. From then on, after Tom completed his work and came home for lunch on a Saturday, he would bring home the company van with the dented ice cream bars and hear the shrieks of delight that echoed along the kopjes as the children screamed, "Ice cream, ice cream," as soon as they saw him arrive.

The following week, we initiated a milk scheme. We bought excess milk and had it delivered to our refrigerator in large steel cans. These we loaded onto the kombis. We went from kraal to kraal, filling containers for the staff, but we had one rule: the children would only get their milk container filled if they themselves drank a glass of it in front of us. Robyn got involved in this work and proved to be very responsible. Lena mostly ignored the entire endeavour. She thought that the only person in need of charity was her. I was constantly surprised at her lack of compassion. She just blotted out anything unpleasant. Robyn was only seven, yet his heart was in the right place.

On the Monday morning, five representatives from Frankenwald went to the meeting with the Witwatersrand chancellor. By that time, the farm manager had arrived home and was generally ignored. When he was accosted about his lack of action in the matter of signing the passes, he shrugged and said, "The kaffirs should have told me. It is all their fault, and they deserved what they got." He showed no remorse. "Those stupid kaffirs …" he said. He did not finish the sentence. One of the younger mess men hit him square on the mouth and laid him out on the kitchen floor.

With these remarks ringing in the representatives' ears, the meeting got underway in the University Chancellor's Office. The Frankenwald representatives stood firm in their resolve. The manager was fired with no references, and the black field staff had their wages increased by the university.

For all the remaining time we stayed at Frankenwald, the children continued to get the ice-cream. The milk scheme was firmly established when my family left for Australia.

The night of the fires was one we would always remember. I recall thinking that I was deathly tired of living in the country of my birth. I did not want to spend my life in pitched battles. I wanted some peace so I could bring up my children and get on with the rest of my life.

I recall thinking that if I did get out and escape to sunnier climes, then I would leave my earlier life locked up in my heart. I knew that I would never come back. And I never have returned. I read the papers today and I am delighted at the rise of the African Middle Class, and at the direction South Africa is heading with people like Mandela leading the way. I feel happy that South Africa is slowly moving to the bright future it deserves.

LIFE CHANGES

Our move to Australia had come at an inauspicious time. We had been trying to leave for a number of years, only to be buffeted by circumstances. You will recall that my dad fell gravely ill and went into hospital. He had been on cortisone to help control his severe sinus problems, but the illness had taken its toll. He had the moon face that bespoke of water retention, and he had grown terribly thin. He finally succumbed to pneumonia and died within four hours right in front of our eyes.

After this devastating loss, we went home silently in Tom's car, opened the front door to Mom's house, and found Chico, our cook, crying his eyes out. We presumed that his tears had to do with my father's demise, but we were wrong. He was clutching the inert body of our Pekinese dog who had fallen ill. Amid the turmoil of my father's death, we had not been aware of the pooch's illness, so we were stunned about the dog's death. My mother, who had not shed a tear so far, pounced on the body of the dead pooch, buried her head in the fur, and sobbed uncontrollably. We told Chico about my father's death. He sat on the kitchen chair and wailed the loss of his best friend, our Pekingese, and the kindest master he had ever had.

Given our circumstances, it was not appropriate for us to leave for Australia. We regrouped and decided to wait a year and see how things went. We rebooked our passage from Durban to Melbourne and went on with our lives. Then, about a month before our sailing date, my grandmother slipped in the bathtub and knocked herself out, breaking several ribs in her fall. She was rushed to hospital, unconscious. Once again, we cancelled the sailing date, as we could not envision leaving Bicha behind in hospital while we took off for down under.

Bicha was in critical care; we organized our schedules to visit her for as long as we could. She was never alone during the day. I would rush to Johannesburg General as fast as I could each day and spend afternoons with her. Then I would rush home and make a meal before Tom and I would rush back with the children in the early evening to sit by Bicha's bedside. She was not improving I dragged my feet at school and went through the motions. I could not conceive of a world without my beloved Bicha in it. I had had dreams of sending for her to join us in Australia. She was not dead, and yet I was mourning her loss already.

On that last Sunday, the entire family assembled. There was great news. Bicha had come out of her coma and was sitting up and talking and paying attention, as if she had only just awakened from a nap. The parking at the hospital grounds was a problem, so Tom let us off and then went with Robyn to a parking lot at the back. We arrived at Bicha's room and were delighted to see her sitting up and in such a jovial mood. She took each one of us in turn and gave us kisses and unusually long hugs.

"But where is Robyn?" she asked. "I shall wait for Robyn." She sat back on her pillows and waited silently. Robyn came bursting into the room. He threw himself at his beloved Bicha. They clung to each other for what seemed a long time. She whispered sweet nothings in his ear. I am sure that, for his part, Robyn knew that he was unconditionally loved by the small, grey-haired woman who had been such a great part of his life. "Look after him always," she said to me. Then she sat back contentedly, sighed, closed her eyes, and died.

Looking back, I can say that, that day had brought me the single most devastating loss in my life. It is strange to relate that I did not cry. I was absolutely numb. The enormity of my loss was like a body blow. I could not feel anything. I recall asking myself why I was not showing any emotion. I felt as if I had been beaten.

Robyn wanted to go to the funeral. I was not sure that this was an appropriate experience for a six-year-old. Still, Robyn borrowed a black tie from his father, got into his white shirt and school jacket, and pronounced that he was ready to go to Bicha's funeral. He held Tom's hand and stood stoically without a tear when he threw soil on the coffin.

It was only when the coffin was lowered that I lost it. It was as if all my feelings had been held back and the dam was about to bust. Looking back over my life from the vantage point of an eighty-year-old, I can still recall that day vividly. Even now, writing about these events that happened so long ago, I still feel deeply the enormity of the loss of the exceptional human being who was my beloved grandmother Bicha.

It is always difficult to recall these traumatic events. I can only say that leaving our home in South Africa was very traumatic on all levels. But staying was not an option. I felt strongly against the apartheid laws. Most of my friends at the university shared my views – in fact, the entire world looked alarmed at the path South Africa was taking.

Bicha was buried only a few feet from my father's grave on a hill in the Clifton Cemetery, on the outskirts of Johannesburg. A brass plate marks her grave. I shall mourn her forever as the most influential person in my life, and I am sure that Robyn will, too. There are times that I feel very alone and want so much to talk to her in the still of the Canadian night.

OLGUICHA

I met her when she was only four years old; I was then eight. She came into my life under strained circumstances, to say the least. In fact, the day a small bed was placed next to mine, her life was in the balance.

Her full name was Olga Helena Pereira Leite, and I wondered how "Pereira" (meaning "pear tree") could give milk ("leite")! The thing I remember most were those huge, soulful brown eyes and her very long, dark brown hair. Her face was a mess of sticking plasters holding threads in place, most of which disappeared down her nose. Her expression was rather forlorn. I noticed that she had thick bandages around her small waist, from which protruded a feeding tube. She looked like an alien from outer space with her swollen body and painfully thin legs.

Her mother put her down on the bed next to mine. Within a few moments, Olga and I were chatting away as if we had known each other forever. We talked about the movies, in particular the new one made by Shirley Temple, our all-time favourite.

I was an only child and was thrilled to have a playmate to talk to. So it was that over the next few days, we cemented a friendship that has lasted over seventy-five years. She slept next to me and I held her hand so that she would know that she was not alone in the dark hours of the night in a house not her own.

Olga and her parents lived in Lourenzo Marques in the Portuguese colony of Mozambique, where her father, an engineer, was the director of railways. Olga had been playing in her parents' backyard the previous week, watching the yard boy clean the back veranda with a pot of lye. She was drawn to the activity by his singing. Many Africans sing animated songs while doing routine jobs. Olga had been drawn to the music and the activity enfolding near the kitchen door. She had, being of a curious nature, unfortunately decided to examine the lye at close quarters. When she saw the whitish powder, she went one further and decided that it might be something edible. She took a large pinch and swallowed.

The results were, without doubt, more disastrous than she ever imagined. She not only burnt her mouth but, in the act of swallowing, had also burnt her oesophagus, all the way down to her stomach. She was rushed to the hospital near her home. Medical facilities in Mozambique were still fairly primitive, so her father had sent her, with her mother, by train over the border to

Johannesburg, where the medical facilities were top-notch. There were no flights in those days between Mozambique and Johannesburg, so Olga and her mother were dispatched by train to see what help might be available for the severely burnt child.

My father, who was in the Portuguese consulate at the time, was alerted to the disaster. He met the train and ushered the mother and child to the hospital, where my mother took up the slack and gave support by providing translation from Portuguese. Olga's mother did not speak much English.

The problem was not readily solved, but the doctors promised to do the best they could with the technology available to them. The first order of business was to provide a means to feed the little girl, so they cut a hole in her stomach wall and attached a wide feeding mouth of rubber. It was through this that Olga was fed a pureed vegetable soup three times a day and a quantity of milk. When she was hungry, she would say that her "tube" was hungry, and she was fed.

The main concern of the doctors was to enlarge the burnt oesophagus over time so that, eventually, Olga would be able to take food again by mouth. They hit on the notion that it would be a great idea to pass a thread down her nose, through the oesophagus and into the stomach, and exiting through the feeding tube to make a complete loop. They then would give her chloroform and thread beads down the loop to keep the burns in the oesophagus open. If the pathways were not kept clear, then Olga would have to live with the feeding tube forever.

Twice a week, she was taken into the operating theatre and given chloroform so that the procedure of pulling the beads through could be undertaken. She would come home dreadfully sick, declaring to all who would listen that her tube was not hungry on that day.

This went on week after week. Olga never cried. She was, for a tiny girl, quite stoic. In all the time that she slept next to me, holding my hand, she never whimpered or felt sorry for herself. I admired her. I wanted to spend all my nights with her hand in mine. I loved her and wanted her to stay in my room forever. She was the sister I never had. One Saturday, I was invited to the theatre to see the latest Shirley Temple film. That day, Olguicha had come out of the hospital looking pale and tormented. I got into her bed and, for the next few hours, discussed the movie I had just seen. I gave her all the excruciating details, and she listened in rapped attention. In fact, it took several nights for me to tell the story.

Olga went home after six months. She was going to have to come back for one final test. If the oesophagus remained open, then she would have the final operation to close her stomach and the wall beneath her ribs so that she would no longer have the "hungry tube" in place. She would have to pay close attention to the size of the morsels she ate for the rest of her life. She would have to come back when she was older to see whether the oesophagus, so badly burnt, had healed enough for her to lead a normal life. All the operations and treatments had been successful.

I cried inconsolably when she left to go home to stay. The nearest thing I had had to a sister was gone forever. I did, when I was a teenager, spend some time with Olguicha in her parents' home in Mozambique during summer vacations. Our friendship carried on as if it had never left off. We still loved each other. I cried when we were separated.

Our paths diverged in adulthood. I went on to university in South Africa. One of my majors was zoology. Olga eventually also went to university, and one of her majors was also zoology! She married an agronomist and had three children. When Mozambique became independent, her family lost not only their father but also all of their material possessions. They fled to Portugal, where they remain to this day.

I recall meeting Olga's much younger brother, Antonio Camilo. He was only about four when I first played with him. We played marbles in the garden, and he screamed with delight when he beat me. I recall his beautiful face, enhanced by the most gorgeous dimples I had ever seen on anyone then – or since.

After I retired, I visited Rio. Olga had alerted her brother that I would be arriving in Brazil. I had never seen Olga's brother as an adult, so I was apprehensive that I might not recognize him. But when I arrived and looked over the crowded barrier at the airport arrivals lounge in Rio, I saw a very tall man with a smile and the most gorgeous dimples I had ever seen. It was instant recognition! He came over and gave me a hug. He looked after me while I was on that vacation in Rio.

Antonio Camilo had practiced law and had immigrated to Brazil after the fall of Mozambique, but he was now retired. We went to the gay-pride parade together during the Carnival festivities. He was a delight. He had married a Belgian woman, a great gal, and they had five children. It was as if I was part of the family. There were no explanations required. We knew all about one another.

But Olga was to come back into my life again, under circumstances that neither of us could ever have foreseen.

In Lisbon, when we were both in our sixties, we spent some time together, as I discovered that Olga had bought an apartment opposite to where my mother was living in retirement. During the first conversation we had when we were reunited after a lifetime, she said that she still remembered in vivid detail the adventures of Shirley Temple in the film I had recounted for her so very long ago!

Our friendship blossomed once again. It was as if we were still in the friendship that had united us so many years ago. She recalled the times we slept holding hands. We still loved each other. She was to prove that, indeed, she would fight for me. In fact, as things turned out, she was probably the only person in my entire life who ever had. After my father died and Tom and I had left South Africa, we wanted to persuade my mother to leave. She held steadfast in her resolve to stay and went on working. She ultimately came to Canada for a visit but was confused by her experiences. She had arrived on South African Airways, from New York to Vancouver but with a stopover in Calgary. It happened to be the time of the Calgary Stampede.

On the plane, my mother noticed that there were, in fact, several cowboys wearing boots with silver stirrups and heading for the stampede shows. Not knowing about the event, my mother concluded that all Americans are, in fact, like in the films – mostly cowboys. She had seen with her own eyes and was a believer. Nothing we said would make her change her mind.

When she arrived in the Vancouver departure hall, it was apparent that she had accidently been disgorged from the plane at the same time as the passengers from a plane from Hong Kong. She looked around. The first words she said to me were, "All the Canadians in Vancouver are Chinese. Why did you not tell me?" It took some explaining to convince her of the multicultural face of Canada.

My mother could have come to Canada, but, for all she talked of "family," she preferred to go back to Lisbon and buy an apartment in a seaside area on the coast north of Lisbon called Carcavelos.

It was a coincidence when she discovered that Olga and her husband, as well as three grown children, lived in an apartment across the street. Olga gave my mother a good deal of support and help. I visited Lisbon to see my mother and was gratified to learn that Olga, her family, and an assortment of their friends had given her a good deal of help. Despite being "home," as Mother put it, the sixty years she had spent in Africa had left their mark. She was estranged on many levels from the ultraconservative society, but most of all she longed to hear English and go to an English library. I sent her English books on tape, as she had cataracts, but she was dragging her feet about having an operation to correct her eyesight. She finally did get her eyes done, but she had a weak heart and had to be careful about her activities.

I was determined to try and get on her emotional level, but it was desperately hard going. She was very critical of me. I do not really know why. I had always been the "good and pleasing child," and my character had been moulded in that direction. However, I had also grown up with fairly enlightened and liberal ideas and an extremely broad education, so that I did not tend to subscribe to the small and petty comments my mother often made. She could not control me, either. I was my own person and had been for most of my life. She bitterly resented that. I proposed that we just love each other, respect each other's ideas, and just be good friends. She stood up and rejected the idea out of hand.

I was her daughter, so there was nothing to discuss! She did not need me as a friend! I was quite upset, but I said nothing. Our relationship remained at status quo. I had planned to stay some time with Mom, but, after ten days or so, I told her that I had to get back home. I bid her adieu, wished her well, and moved across town into a hotel, where I breathed a sigh of relief.

Many years previous, in the process of becoming a child psychologist, I was told that my character was heavily grounded on being "good" in order to please an "unpleasable" mother. I was an intrusion in the tight hold she had on my father. She had always become angry when I did well and my father praised me. As I got older, I mistakenly thought that if I achieved, then my mother would be pleased. I was terribly wrong. She loved to show off my achievements to others, but she deeply resented them. Looking back, I can see that she had not had the opportunities I had been granted, and so, with me, she felt herself on shifting sand. I often contradicted her erroneous ideas, and this made her furious.

So, right up to old age, my mother remained the controlling and, to me, unlikable person that she was. I was not too concerned, for I had had a deeply emotionally tie to my loving and generous-spirited grandmother, whom I had adored. She had been my mother figure, and I had practically nothing to do with my own mother, who, for reasons of her own, wanted me out of sight and out of mind.

After some time, Mom developed heart problems that were fairly serious. She went into hospital for a lengthy stay. I flew over to be with her. She was not pleased to see me. She insisted that I take her home immediately. The doctor recommended against it, so I refused to do it. She sulked. I stayed in the apartment. There were fierce rainstorms that infiltrated the outer wall of the kitchen and inundated the kitchen itself. The kitchen drain was blocked and made a terrible mess: carpets soaked and puddles everywhere. My mother wanted to come home. I told her that the apartment was uninhabitable, especially for one straight out of hospital. She shouted, sulked, and led me in a merry dance. She was going to get a taxi and go home. The doctor advised her to go home by ambulance and said that the apartment needed to be fixed before she attempted the journey. He suggested that she might try a *lar,* a home for the aged where she could be looked after, fed, and given her medication. She refused and then screamed at me. At this stage, I was beginning to be unperturbed by her ravings. I determined that she would only return to her apartment when the builders had finished their work.

I took my mother by ambulance to a Home near where she lived. It was temporary: a few days at most. She was in a room with another woman who was quite ill. As the other woman did not speak English, I suggested that it might be better if Mother and I spoke English together so that our conversations would be private. To spite me, she started screaming in Portuguese, telling everyone that I was a terrible daughter and that I was keeping her from her home. After a few hours of abuse, and once the staff brought her meal and her medication, I left. I was emotionally exhausted. I sat in a park nearby and cried. Then I composed myself and went home to continue the rescue from the wet. The builders had left a terrible mess. The kitchen was no longer under water, and the outer wall was now repaired so that no further rains would penetrate. I threw out the bedroom carpets, but the dining and living room carpets were still soaked. I tried to get somebody to come to collect them, wring out the water, and dry them out.

The next day, my mother was not talking to me and was readying herself to leave the home in a taxi. I told her that I needed another day to dry the carpeting, but she was having none of it. In any case, she had fought with the staff, telling them that the bathroom was very dirty and that she was not used to this kind of thing. She was impossible if thwarted. There was no consoling her. The doctor came to visit. He laid down the law. Mum negotiated with the doctor to go home in two days. She sulked when she saw me, accusing me of putting her in the home to get rid of her. She was totally irrational. I bore the brunt of all her bad temper tantrums.

I went home to clean up and make the place liveable. Even the bath was a mess, it was full of the builders' garbage, which had not been collected. I bought food, made beds, and tried to make things presentable for my mother's homecoming.

The day I called for her, she was not talking to me. She ignored me mostly. Strutting into her apartment, she said, "It is all lies. There is nothing wrong. You just did not want me to come home." I put her to bed and said nothing.

I was apprehensive that when I went home to Canada, my mother might not be able to cope – and putting her into a home was out of the question. The home we had previously arranged for her would, under no circumstances, take her back anyway.

I consulted with Olguicha, and we decided that perhaps we should cast about to see whether we could get some older women to come and live in and accept the responsibility of cooking for and looking after my mother – a sort of paid companion. I knew the pitfalls. If it was a woman of some education, then my mother would feel threatened; if it was not, then my mother would not heed her and would treat her like a servant.

"What I need is a black woman," my mother said. What she failed to understand was that she was no longer in South Africa and that humble, obsequious servants were increasingly hard to find!

I flew back to my Florida beach-house. Olga managed to get my mother a live-in companion, a middle-class woman who had been widowed and had had a brain tumour but was now recovering. My mother tolerated the companion for a week and then fired her. This meant that Olga had to check in on her regularly, all the while pretending not to do so. A year later, the hospital phoned me to tell me that my mother had arrived alone in the hospital at midnight in an ambulance and had died at three in the morning, quite peacefully. I had feelings of relief. I was not going to miss her. It was as if a giant cloud had been moved out of my horizon. I felt sorry for my mother and asked a close childhood friend, Joao, to arrange the ceremonies at the church and the internment. I saw to it that my mother had everything she would have wanted, but I did not attend.

Later, I went to Lisbon to dispose of my mother's furniture and give her personal attire to an eighty-year-old distant relative. All I have of hers is one of her books by Somerset Maughan, which I had so enjoyed in my youthful years.

Olga and her family moved back to Portugal to a family farm that had belonged to them for aeons. She had three children, had become a teacher, and made a life for herself. We continued the friendship we had started as children so long ago. Last year, we went on a cruise together. She is still my closest friend.

There was a major problem when it came to getting the passport that I needed in order to travel to Australia. I had always had a Portuguese passport even though I was born in South Africa. I was married to a Canadian, but, according to law, I was not able to assume Canadian nationality until I had lived in Canada for at least a year. The Canadians could not issue me papers. The Portuguese had some archaic laws which decreed that once a Portuguese woman was married to a foreign national, she could no longer claim Portuguese nationality.

The only option was for me to suddenly become a South African national. But even this was fraught with problems. The government decreed that those wishing to leave their native country were to be considered traitors and would be scrutinized to determine whether a passport should be issued at all. "A passport is a privilege and not a right" was the official policy. The fact of the matter was that I was stateless … I felt like an orphan. I was determined not to apply for a South African passport under these or any other circumstances.

The day for our departure loomed, and still I had no papers. Just before he died, my father had, unbeknownst to me, signed documents to allow me to keep my original Portuguese nationality. Sometime after his death, I was summoned to the consulate and told that there was a passport for me, issued in my maiden name and signed by my father, with the signature and seals he normally used when issuing such documents. He had saved the day.

I was cleaning out some papers from my safe forty years later, and the old passport came to light. I have kept it and treasured it all my life. I can still read my father's signature as the issuing consular representative. It was his last and most memorable gift to me. He had set me free.

$$* \quad * \quad *$$

So it was that Tom, the children, and I bid a tearful farewell to our friends and to my mother. She was now alone. She had, in a short space of time, lost her mother, her husband, and now Tom, Robyn, and me. Made of stern stuff, she was planning to retire to Lisbon, where she would return to live after being away for forty years. She had continued to work in the consulate as a consular secretary and appeared to enjoy her work. It filled her days, gave her companionship, and kept her in contact with the Portuguese community in which she had spent her days.

It became increasingly clear that my daughter, Lena, would have her schooling disrupted if she went with us to Australia at this juncture. She was in her last years of schooling, studying for her matriculation, or university entrance, exam. She had a great deal of work ahead of her, but we could no longer afford to postpone our trip. Having waited for three years and postponed our departure four times, we felt it was now or never. Lena was to live with a girlfriend in the apartment next door to my mother's place. This way, her grandmother could keep an eye on her.

Finally, the day came when we left Frankenwald, a place we loved and where we all had learnt extraordinary life lessons.

The three of us caught the P&O Liner from Durban and watched the African coast disappear on the horizon that morning in 1965. We knew that it might be a lifetime before anyone of us ever came back, if at all. A turbulent chapter in our lives was closed, but a new one was about to begin in the far land called "Down Under."

GOING DOWN UNDER

For many years, Tom received letters from his hockey-playing teammates telling him what they were doing with their lives. One of the friends he most admired had gone to settle in Australia. He wrote glowing reports of the country, its people, and the potential opportunities for good employment.

The decision was made to leave South Africa, where life had become increasingly untenable. Tom decided that Australia would provide the best opportunities for resettlement. I, on the other hand, had mixed feelings about it. It seemed to me that I would be going to the back of beyond and that, apart from the weather, which was similar to that of South Africa, Australia did not have a great deal to recommend it, apart from many wide-open spaces, gum trees, and millions of sheep.

I had wanted Tom to return home to Canada. Canada appealed to me on many levels. With the exception of the cold and snowy climate, it seemed, from my perspective, to be a progressive country with ideologies and a way of life into which I could settle very comfortably.

Tom shrugged off the positive comments and reiterated his belief that in Canada there were but two options: "One could starve to death or freeze to death." It must be understood that Tom had been a teenager during the Depression. His family had had a terrible time. Living in Saskatchewan during those bleak days, he had to leave school to help support his family when his father, who worked on the Canadian Railways, was allowed to work only one day a week. The family lost everything. Tom had to endure the harshness of the prairie winters in flimsy clothes and often with shoes that did not keep out the wet.

He had become the helper to an old man who had an old cart from which he sold frozen fish from door to door. Tom's mother had a hard time feeding the family, so, with a terribly guilty conscience, Tom stole one fish a day by throwing it into a snow bank. Later, he would retrieve it, and the Durling family would have a meal. It bothered Tom a great deal to do this, especially as the old man had become a friend. Tom was torn inside and vowed that as soon as he was able, he would repay his debt. It was two years later when Tom tried to find his old friend. By that time, Tom was playing hockey and earning some money at it. He went to his old friend's house to find that he had died the previous winter, so he told the family that he owed them some money, left an envelope with the cash, and did not give them any details. At least he could go forward with a clear conscience.

The Durling family decided that things in Canada were not getting any better and that their situation was growing steadily worse. They decided to return home to England and start a new life. There, at least, they would have family around them. Tom's older brother Joe went with them and was responsible for his parents' welfare.

Tom had become an excellent hockey player and was able to earn a living playing the game. He was in the team that played for Canada when they won the World Games. He coached various leagues and travelled hither and thither to play matches. He loved to travel. It became his raison d'être.

I knew that Tom had been deeply scarred in his teen years by his experiences in the Depression. He never again felt secure. Even in times when he was earning good money, he always kept a stash of cash in his trunk – "just in case." I suspect that having a family increased his anxiety. I also know that he was pleased when I completed my studies and started to have earning potential; he did not want my money, just peace of mind. The Depression had left large scars in his unconscious. I have a feeling that this insecurity was, in part, responsible for his not marrying earlier. The fact that I had the potential to earn a good salary let him sleep nights. But he was misguided. Australia was the last place a woman could earn a decent wage, as I was to learn, much to my chagrin.

Tom had done well in South Africa. He was the general manager of Lever Brothers there. Part of him wanted to stay and continue in the job he liked and where he was treated with much consideration by the people in London, who came out periodically to oversee the operation. But life in South Africa had become untenable, so we caught the P&O Liner out of Southampton and travelled via Cape Town and Durban to Perth, Melbourne, and Sydney in 1965.

* * *

We left from Durban in the summer and went directly out over the Indian Ocean, which has no ports of call, and on to Freemantle in Western Australia. Every day, we awoke to the endless expanses of a featureless ocean.

We enjoyed the fact that, for once, we had no duties to attend to. We could spend days doing absolutely nothing. Or, if the spirit moved us, we could take part in the planned activities on board.

Robyn was in heaven. We did not impose on him the strict exigencies of daily life that we had on land. There was no school and no lessons. He could stay up as late as he wished and sleep in as long as he pleased. We let him set his own times as the spirit moved him, for the first time in his life. He chose to hang out with the orchestra. He spent time at rehearsal and was befriended by members of the band. Tom would take a plate of eggs and toast and a glass of milk up to the cabin at about nine o'clock, after we had had our breakfast, shake Robyn, and then feed him breakfast. The boy often ate without even opening his eyes, as if resenting the intrusion. Finally, with the last mouthful, he would roll over and continue to sleep, dreaming, no doubt, about his merry late nights with the band and its music.

We decided to indulge Robyn because he had just received several great blows in his young life. The first was the death of his beloved great-grandmother, whom he loved to distraction, just as I had always done all my life. His grandfather also died quite suddenly, a short time afterwards. Then, with our trip out to a distant land, Robyn had left both his sister and grandmother behind. He had lost his carefree existence at Frankenwald and the companionship of the little black football players in the grassy patch every day after school. His small world had suddenly changed drastically. We took all this into account and were indulgent.

Apart from gravitating automatically to anyone who could play a tune, Robyn would also make conversation with elderly white-haired women he perceived as grandmotherly. He carried their parcels, made intelligent small talk, and sat next to them when they ordered tea.

Later, while exploring South Island, New Zealand, Robyn's relationship with one elderly woman really blossomed. He asked whether he could sit on the tour bus with his new granny – a white-haired Australian from Adelaide. Then, each morning, he would help her on the bus, carry her bag, and strap on a toy pistol to his waist in order to protect her from any threat.

On one occasion, he asked me whether he could sleep in her room. "She needs me to help her," he said. I did not want Rob to impose on his friend, so I approached her to ask if he would be a nuisance. She said that she would love it and gave him a hug. For the rest of the trip through South Island, all the way to Invercargill, and back, Robyn roomed at night with his Australian grandmother. He carried her bags, tucked her in, ordered and poured her endless cups of tea, and entertained her on the bus by sitting next to her and occasionally holding her hand. I knew that Rob was finding comfort where he could after the tremendous loss of a beloved great-grandmother whom he loved deeply and who had left an indelible mark on his soul.

Our first port of call was Freemantle. We took a bus into the capital, Perth for our first glimpse of Australia. Perth was a beautiful, clean city on a hill, boasting numerous green spaces and the first black swans I had ever seen. It was also on the ocean, which, for me, had great appeal. I decided to pop into the psychological services of the education department for a chat. I explained that my family and I were going to explore the other cities in Oz but that we might decide eventually to come back to Perth, as we liked what we had seen so far. "Would you be interested in employing me?" I asked. The answer was affirmative. They wanted to know if I would communicate with them if I decided to settle in Perth. I promised that I would.

Tom and I, once in Melbourne, decided to leave the ship. It was not that we were thinking of settling in Melbourne itself; it was merely that the geographical location was strategic and handy for exploring this vast country. It was close to Sydney and Adelaide, and a hop, skip, and a jump to Tasmania. We also wanted to explore the coasts of New South Wales and Queensland. The barrier reef was the pièce de résistance, so we were determined to leave its exploration to a later time, when we had settled on a place to live.

It was a strange arrangement, our arrival in Melbourne. We were permitted to leave the ship, but our luggage would only be disgorged onto the pier the following day. We thought it prudent to find a hotel almost immediately. Having no insight into the city, we presumed (incorrectly, as it turned out) that hotels near the beach were probably fairly good. Tom got us a large room with three beds, all with huge dents in the middle and covered with thin chenille bedspreads that had seen better days. The pillows had to be handled with care, as they had unstitched seams; the feathers had a habit of flying all over the place, much to Rob's delight. I did not know then about Australian bathrooms. These are generally located on a veranda. True to form, we had a very ancient spindly bathtub with claw-and-ball feet and a dripping tap that refused to deliver more than a drip at a time. When the water would complain bitterly by making unseemly noises inside the pipes, the pipes would shake and vibrate so much that I am sure the other tenants heard them.

Bathrooms never had toilets. These were located in the far reaches of a balcony or on the back porch of many houses. I soon learnt that asking to use the bathroom would meet one with uncomprehending stares! Toilet paper was also scarce. There were neat little stacks of cut-up newspapers usually stuck on nails in the door.

Everywhere we travelled, getting hot water was always a problem. Nobody had figured out that hot water meters that accepted coins should be located in bathrooms. They were invariably either in the corridor outside or on the back porch. We three would huddle in the bathroom while Tom, scantily dressed for the occasion, popped in the required coins to get the gas heater going. Robyn and I would have to make a dash. "There is no time to wash around the ears," complained Robyn. He was right. We had to be careful not to be left all soaped over. In that event, it was then only possible to go out again and feed more coins into the meter in order to complete one's wash. Tom would stand by at the ready, coins in hand. When the water was about to gurgle into drips, he would stoke the proverbial fires, go out into the corridor, and then dash in and try to wash as rapidly as possible. We would often be caught, and so I would dash out in a state of undress to help Tom complete his battle for hot water. It was hilarious. We all laughed long and hard, but the locals were quite upset by the fact that we thought all this quaint. They, having to live with this modus operandi everywhere – in the city and beyond – were offended at out critical remarks. After all, they quipped, "What do you know?" We were only, as they put it, new migrants.

On our third day in Melbourne, our luggage arrived from the pier by horse and cart. The poor swayback horse looked tired, while his driver, a fat roly-poly Queenslander with an accent that one could cut with a knife, helped us move into our new small flat. We had found this accommodation in a hurry. It was in the district of St Kilda, close to the hotel where we had stayed on our first night in this new land. It was only to be a temporary move. We could laugh at the quaint accommodation it provided while trying to regroup and deciding what to do next. Our first priority was to get Rob into school. I enrolled him to the local elementary school, where he was taught by a wonderful male teacher whom I much admired, once I got to know him.

Our St Kilda apartment was not so much an apartment as a remodelled part of an enormous old house that had seen better days. There were two-tier indented beds in an attic bedroom covered with the ubiquitous chenille bedspreads in a vomit colour. A small folded bed was placed between our beds. There, Rob was very happy to be able to stretch out at night and hold our hands when he needed reassurance.

Our small apartment in the big house in St Kilda introduced us to a bevy of interesting characters, the likes of which we had never met, before or since.

The owner of this rambling house was a tough, short, red-haired confirmed bachelor from the outback. He had made a little money and retired to live out his days in the front room of his house, one replete with French doors leading out onto a red-brick-floor-covered veranda. He could always be found sitting and chain-smoking at his large desk. He would be there all day, it seemed, listening to the "gigis"(horses)and betting on all the races at tracks all over Australia. He had meals brought to the desk and ate alone, with only the drone of the racing commentators for company. By mid-afternoon, he usually had too many beers under his belt and could not carry on a conversation without slurring. He was always cheery and affable, if not always coherent.

Then there was the housekeeper, Alice. She lived with her family in the front room of the house and ran the cleaning and tidying operations. A thin, self-effacing woman of about fifty, she had the air of one whose life had been only a series of hard labours. She had two children, one of them a girl much like her mother in appearance and disposition and with an equally self-effacing character. I could never get a word out of her. Her son was quite tall and would have been pleasant-looking except that he was always in a slouch, never looked one in the face, and slunk away whenever one attempted conversation. He reminded me of Uriah Heep.

Their abode, the great room of what must have originally been the parlour of a great house, had a huge fireplace (unused) and a big double bed with a bright pink chenille bedspread. There were two screens, behind which I presumed lived the daughter and Uriah Heep.

Alice busied herself in a small "copper room" in the back. I had never seen one of these coppers in operation before, and, in fact, had not known of their existence. The contraptions were large cauldrons (made of copper, of course) with an added feature: a portion on the base was arranged so as to hold small logs to make the fire. Laundry was not washed. It was boiled, often for hours at a time. Doing the laundry seemed to consume much of Alice's day. She kept the fire fed and the washing turned by hand till her loads were done.

In the back garden was the ubiquitous dunny with its inevitable supply of carefully cut newspaper on the proverbial spike in the door, which had been cobbled together with planks so that one could peep in to ascertain whether it was in use or not.

In the back, too, was a small room that was difficult to call a kitchen. It was difficult to swing the proverbial cat in there, but Alice had been able to do this for the better part of thirty years. The kitchen had a coal stove, plus a small food cupboard attached at a crazy angle to the wall.

It was Alice's job to put her employer to bed each night, as, by that point, he was in no condition to go anywhere without considerable help. Just how she managed this I was not certain, as she must have had to carry more than twice her weight.

Then there was Alice's husband, Joe. He was the strong and silent type and did not encourage conversation at first. He got to know me, as I always made a point of talking to him. I gathered that he worked in the Melbourne municipality in the transport division. He was very proud of his profession, one of which I had hitherto never heard. He left early every morning to go perform his allotted task, carrying with a large black pot filled with what appeared to be pitch but proved to be black grease. He was to spend his days walking around the track intersections of the Melbourne trams, applying a little grease here and there. I once managed to engage him in conversation. He seemed to be severely limited in his perspectives, but he beamed when he confided that he had the best job in the world – and the best job he had ever had. It is a case of different strokes for different folks. I was about to ask him about other jobs he had worked, but I felt that I better leave well alone.

As soon as we had settled in the old house with our new companions and Rob had gone to school, Tom found himself a job as a shipping clerk. He was delighted. This was going to be fun. His wages were paid in cash in an envelope every second week. I had no opportunity to do anything. I found myself grounded with a severe bout of flu, a wickedly sore throat, and no voice. I could hardly go and apply for a job under these circumstances.

It took me almost two weeks to feel human again, at which time I started to make plans to go to the Commonwealth Employment Agency in order to apply for some routine job. I knew that if I went to the Professional Services Bureau, I would have to take things seriously and do the job for which I had been trained. As a psychologist, I had to sign a contract, and that was the one thing I did not want to do as yet. We wanted to fill in time and go exploring whenever Rob had school holidays. After all, we had not seen anything of this huge country. Our explorations were merely local and confined largely to places along the tram routes.

I left my certificates at home and went for a job interview. Things did not go well. What was I skilled to do? I had not figured out any lies to obfuscate the truth. Could I at least type? There were openings as dish washers and assistant cooks, also counter clerks.

I kept admitting that I would probably be terrible at any of those jobs. "Then what *can* you do?" asked the irate counsellor. I broke down and told him that I was a teacher with a specialty in the area of children with neurological disorders and also that I was a child psychologist. I said all this somewhat apologetically.

"Why, then, are you wasting my time?" he roared. He picked up the phone and, in two seconds, arranged for a suitable interview in the professional division. I had not wanted to do this at all, but I had no way of going back. I felt cornered. I went home, brought out my degree certificates, and caught the tram to the interview that had been set up without my consent. I hoped that I might still be able to get out of it.

Within the first five minutes, the counsellor called the principal from the school for the deaf. Within ten, I had a job description: "the assessment of all the children in the Melbourne School for the Deaf." No one in Oz was trained to do this. I signed a contract for a year with the psychological services (which I had been trying to avoid like the plague). By then, there was no respite and no going back.

Welcome to our first month down under!

*   *   *

Once Tom and I had jobs and Robyn was in school, we decided to rent a more modern apartment. I found a small unfurnished place. This was no problem, as we had come equipped with camp beds and sleeping bags. We had a regular camping table which unfolded and sprouted four attached seats. We had camping kitchen utensils and pots, so we were in business. In very short order, we were comfortable. We had only the necessities, but we were happy.

We soon found that our neighbours were two young gay men who alternated between kissing and hugging in the stairwell and fighting, which consisted of kicking each other and screaming obscenities on the landing. Robyn, who had never been exposed to this kind of adult interaction, was abashed and flabbergasted. "What is their problem?" he asked. At his age, I did not feel that a full explanation was a good idea, so I told him that they were badly behaved adults who should have known better.

Another neighbour was a young policeman in training who lived with his mother. He had taken an interest in Robyn, and Robyn was proud to have a "cop" for a buddy.

Over the back fence of the apartment block was a large, rambling "Ozzie Queenslander" replete with climbing roses and the inevitable veranda all around the perimeter of the house. It was owned by a noisy couple. They did not appear during the day and confined their altercations to the wee hours of the morning. The woman was a bartender and, as far as I could tell, always on the border of inebriation. She had a jealous Greek husband who worked days and waited for his wife to get home in order to continue the battle. They swore and shouted, loud crashes resounding in the night. Some nights, the rows were so bad as to merit the interference of the apprentice cop, who would storm over the fence and threaten them with the full force of the law if they continued to disturb the peace. There would be silence for a couple of nights until something tipped the balance and they were off again doing battle.

On the positive side, I was enjoying making friends with the staff in the offices of the psyche services. Two colleagues offered (and we accepted) the loan of two armchairs, which had been in someone's attic. Tom went downtown to purchase a hi-fi so we could listen to classical music. We were feeling positively luxurious! I am always surprised at how very little one really needs in order to be happy.

I made good use of the trams, going from one assessment to another, but, mainly, I worked with adolescents, trained in the school for the deaf, and saw new cases in the school for spastics. I came home at four o'clock, and then Robyn and I waited for Tom to arrive so we could explore a different part of the city.

We hated the climate. It was like nothing we had been exposed to before. In the balmy days of summer, the temperature would soar into the stratosphere. People around us had houses decorated and closed to avoid the Melbourne chill. Curtains of velvet were common, and sliding windows were often nailed shut. The result was that the homes were claustrophobic. No matter, the inhabitants seemed to have found respite. They would take blow-up mattresses to the beaches and lie in the shallow water, allowing the tide to cool their bodies. There would be hundreds of mattresses on the beach on a blistering night.

It was also common for Melbourne to be confused about the seasons. Temperatures could move sixty degrees in one day! When I was informed of this probability, I thought that the person was pulling my leg. But one very cold morning in summer, I went to work with a polo-neck sweater and a wool suit. By lunchtime, I was melting; by three in the afternoon, I was suffocating. I rushed home to put on a thin cotton shirt and matching pants. I then went off to the store to buy something for dinner. Within the hour, it was again so cold that I was shuddering and had to run home, as the wind was freezing.

The residents of Melbourne would tell newcomers that the Yarra River was the only river in Oz that actually ran "upside down"! It was terribly muddy and grey-brown in colour from all the silt carried along. It did look like a transient mud puddle.

We often walked down to the waterfront to watch the gulls. But even these had a terrible time. The wind would blow so hard that they had to counterbalance and seemed always to be sitting at an angle, with their feathers ruffled, and definitely not enjoying the cold winds.

Melbourne prided itself on being the most culturally sophisticated City in Australia. It was probably true. There was a snobbishness and an air of being more British than the British they were emulating. Little Collins Street could easily have been in England.

I recall that during those halcyon days I developed a severe toothache. I went to a dentist whom someone recommended, the only one who would take me at short notice. He proved to be a German from the Rhineland. He was large, portly, and terribly arrogant. He refused to give me an injection of Novocain. I refused to let him do the procedure without it, as I was in enough pain as it was!

He bellowed at me and tried to bully me. I just refused to cooperate. I was near tears, as I hate confrontations of any kind, never having had to deal with them in my life. I sat firm while the dentist stamped his foot and blared at me in German, occasionally saying, "Mein Gott," and other epithets I could not place. He was not going to give up, but then neither was I. I was made of stronger mettle.

He stormed out into the inner sanctum, where he continued to bellow at his nurse, while I detached myself from the chair and made a hasty exit to the street. I noticed from the building directory that there was a clutch of dentists on the upper floor of the same building. I rushed up, looking pale and wan. Would they take care of an ailing "migrant"? They did, and soon the offending tooth was filled and I went home with no pain and a feeling of vindication.

On the Easter holiday, we flew to New Zealand, where one of Tom's friends from his hockey days lived. I loved New Zealand from the start. What wonderful people and glorious scenarios! No acute climatic variations here! We began to wonder whether we had made the right decision to settle in Australia. New Zealand appealed to me so much more for innumerable reasons, not the least of which was that I was offered a job at the University of Wellington. We flew back to Oz, mulling it over.

* * *

It turned out that we spent a year in Melbourne. I had to fulfil my contract, so Tom and I worked while Robyn attended the local elementary school.

Every school vacation and every long weekend, we went off exploring. We got to know the province of Victoria fairly well. We also travelled south to Phillip Island. Many Australians had holiday homes there. I was disappointed in that many of the holiday homes were, in effect, more or less shacks – untidy, unkempt, haphazard, and downright ugly. In most, there was no running water. They would have been more elegant had they been replaced by holiday tents. But we were not there to admire the scenery.

We stayed long enough to see the beautiful little penguins that staggered onto the island to spend the night. We were given a seat on a small beach where the sea pounded the coastline. We waited for the allotted time when the first wet, sleek heads appeared, replete with flapping flippers. From the darkness, the lights were suddenly turned on, and we could see the small creatures fighting the rough waters of the relentless sea and then flopping, exhausted, on the sand of the cove. They picked themselves up, shook themselves off, and waddled the walk of the exhausted to their small enclaves, where they spent the night. It was a sight I would always remember.

I drove to Ballarat, north of Melbourne, to do some work in the residential school for the deaf in that city. I liked the countryside. It was lush and had many vineyards. The city had an air of gentility that would have sat well in the English countryside.

We took ten days to travel by car to the coast and then took a ferry to Tasmania, a beautiful little island with miles and miles of hops, which are grown there to enhance the beer industry. The southernmost part of the island is wild and free. It is a national park and, as such, has been left in its natural state. The waves and the wind beat relentlessly on the side exposed to the Antarctic waters, and huge storms formed the trees into grotesque shapes. This was the area reputed to be home to the mythical Tasmanian tiger. But this animal was now thought to be extinct, as it was pursued and slaughtered by arrogant hunters ever since the English convicts arrived in Australia.

We visited a sanctuary in Melbourne where there was the almost extinct lyrebird. It was about the size of a seagull, delicate in appearance with beige muted feathers. It moved slowly. I could see that it was easy prey in the wild and probably did not have the smarts to stay away from its most ferocious enemy, humankind.

We drove to the Dandenongs, the mountains behind Melbourne, and admired the interesting vegetation there, where it seemed, at first glance, that the large trunks with hairy tops were trees turned upside down. We saw towering mountain ash trees, massive tree ferns, and rampant creepers. The views of the sprawling city to the west were breathtaking. It felt as if we had arrived in fairyland.

When I finally told the psychology department that I was going to move on and that I and my husband had decided to go cross-country to Western Australia, the department head was nice enough to phone Perth, talk to the psych services there, and give me a great recommendation. I phoned Western Australia to confirm that I would be coming to Perth to settle, and they told me that when I arrived, I would have a job waiting for me.

We had a going-away party in our miniscule apartment, where I provided the food and everyone else brought something to sit on and their own plate and cutlery. Despite the apparent limitations, it turned out to be one of the best parties that I had ever been to, lasting till the wee hours of the morning.

The following day, we packed our meagre belongings into our small car and went off towards Sydney via the Lakes Entrance area. We were self-sufficient. We had a large tent and our usual beds and sleeping bags. Cooking was a problem because of the flies. I had not realized that in the outlying areas, the land was abuzz with big, lethargic brown flies. Everywhere, pictures of the outback look wild and enticing, but the reality is that beating off these lethargic and ever-present beasties is no laughing matter. These flies were not like any I had encountered previously. They were larger, for a start, and clung onto clothing as one moved about, refusing to be shaken off.

Making breakfast in the entrance of our tent was a matter of speed and ambush. We closed all possible vents and openings. I fried the breakfast eggs with the speed of lightning and had the family stand in line with plates at the ready, while Tom held a fly swatter in hand; I did not dilly-dally. We ate as fast as we could without causing acute indigestion and slurped our coffee holding a hand over the top of the cup so that flies would not accidently drown in it. We washed the plates and put them away immediately; only then could we open the tent up to let in the day. Lakes Entrance is beautiful and wild. I did not much enjoy the camping. It was always disorganized, and the campers did not seem to respect the spaces of other campers.

Whenever groups got together, the drinking would start. It would go on all night, getting rowdier and rowdier so that sleep was impossible. The first morning, we found a youth nestled under our tent, dead drunk. Nobody seemed to mind. We found that we did not enjoy the company of the other campers, as, to them, holidays meant a time to let loose and let it all hang out for as long as one could maintain a state of complete inebriation. It was not only the men. I found a woman on a washroom floor dead to the world and "sleeping it off."

We entered Sydney and made for the house in Manly belonging to a South African family, great friends of my best friend Freda from my university days. Molly had four children, and her husband was a professor in the engineering department of the University of New South Wales. They had left South Africa for the same reasons we had and were having a difficult time settling in. Molly's house was being built around her. As she and her husband had little money, she was mainly building it. She felt ambivalent about the Australian way of life and, like me, hated the culture of the endless beer drinking and the fact that anyone not taking alcohol was thought to be not only positively strange but also positively lacking as a human being!

Tom was only interested in the odd glass of wine. I was allergic to alcohol. From a young age, I discovered that even a small amount of alcohol would give me pains in the kidneys, inspire a crushing migraine, and make me start to vomit. I had no hard feelings about alcohol itself, but I would weasel my way around any social situation where drinking was de rigueur. I did not drink anything, anytime, anywhere. I was happy to offer guests a drink, as long as I did not have to join them.

We rented an Aussie trailer. Having previously looked at some, we determined that, frankly, the Australians had no idea what a camper should be like. We looked at several dealerships and finally settled for what we could get. The camper was poorly designed. The two beds provided were stuffed in such a way that they slanted outwards, so it was easy to end up turning over in the night and falling on the carpet! The sink had a piece of tubing leading to a bucket, and the water tank had to be filled constantly when in place and then emptied for travel.

I was beginning to get a picture of the Australian character. Anything artistic was put down as useless, and there was no regard for aesthetics. I have never seen such appallingly put-together house décor as I saw in Australia. I did notice that once the master of the house bought "his" chair to sit in, it would be there forever. The material would fade and the stuffing would come out. When it needed replacement, a bath towel was arranged over the seat and be held together with large safety pins. The chair would continue in use as if there were a social contract signed and sealed for it to be there, in all its ugliness, forever in the parlour.

When we were living in Perth, I laughed at the controversy raging over the building of the Sydney Opera House. It was too expensive; it was being built by a foreigner; why would Ozzies need such a useless thing as an opera house? I never met anyone who was in favour of its being built. The Scandinavian architect left the building unfinished and went home in disgust before it had been completed. There were huge cost overruns, and there were screaming debates in Parliament. Today, it is considered one of the only outstandingly beautiful buildings in Australia, a landmark embellishing the Sydney waterfront and known all over the world. Most Ozzies kicked and screamed foul in all the years it had taken to complete the structure. One man told me that it looked like an old typewriter filled with shells.

The one outstanding characteristic of the Australian psyche is a desire to pull down, demean, and reduce everything to the lowest common denominator. Expertise, achievement, and beauty had to be joked about and denigrated. It was imperative that everyone should "fit in" and that there be no acknowledgement of social class or individual endowments. Anyone showing any special expertise had to be brought down to the level where his or her abilities would be trashed. People felt that they had to hide their abilities or else be ostracized. I saw my well-educated colleagues slouch into grammatical errors and remove from their speech any "descriptive" words for fear of appearing "uppity."

Many new English immigrants had been schooled in good English and grammar, and for this reason they would be made fun of, unmercifully.

Men wanted to remain "rough" and spent hours and hours socializing with their mates in the local pub. The women were home with the children and had to wait in line to be noticed. For many years, they were not even permitted to enter the saloons the men frequented. There were ladies' parlours set aside for women's exclusive use. For the men, drinking-mates were the ones that counted. The Shielas were merely something to be tolerated at home in exchange for sexual favours. The status of women was at a very low ebb. It is no accident that Germaine Greer came from Melbourne.

I had once waited till after working hours to speak to a man who had a spastic child in very poor health. Recommendations had to be made for her future. It was appropriate for both parents to be enrolled in these discussions. Dad arrived at six o'clock in ill humour. "What do you want to see me for?" he asked. "After all, it is 'er kid!" He refused to sit down. I could not get his attention. He was distracted and told his wife that he would see her after he got home from the pub!

* * *

We spent a week exploring Sydney, but, apart from the Sydney Harbour Bridge, the endless gum trees, and the row houses reminiscent of Plymouth in England, we felt it was all too busy, noisy, and brash.

We drove north to Queensland, the Province I most enjoyed. The climate is perfect, with a mild winter and balmy summers. The city was developed on the banks of the river and thirty miles from the sea. This land exceeded my expectations. I was excited by the visions of the trees with enormous coloured flowers, only to find that when we approached, the "flowers' were an illusion. In fact, they were brightly coloured parakeets who took off in clouds.

We had driven up the coast from Sydney and camped at small villages such as Nowra, where Tom and Rob found a fishing pier and we spent a day resting and awaiting a fish dinner. I had stayed home to wash my hair and do the laundry. I sauntered down to where the boys were casting their lines off a small pier. They had caught nothing as yet, but were very serious about their endeavours. I was bored, so, after a while, I found a piece of fishing line and put a small hook with a scrap of bait on the end. I let it dangle off the jetty. It took only a couple of minutes before I screamed with delight and pulled out a good-sized fish. Tom and Rob were crestfallen, and I was stunned. I had spoilt their day and stolen their thunder, quite by accident. Robyn was cross and would not talk to me. I promised not to go fishing with them ever again. But we had fresh fish for supper!

We could not dally too long. Having caught a glimpse of Brisbane, I was sorry to have to hurry back to Melbourne. Our time was short. I made a note that Queensland was a place I would like to explore further. We revelled in the glorious beaches of the Gold Coast, but, socially speaking, things in Melbourne were generally much behind South Africa. Melbourne was, for all its faults, a place where people had regard for intellectual pursuits, where theatre and the arts were appreciated. This could not be said of the other places we visited. The big consideration, however, was the climate – and the Melbourne climate had nothing to recommend it. Having been born in South Africa with its fabulous climate, I often tended to view other places with a jaundiced eye when making a comparison.

At the end of the academic year, Tom prepared for us to make the journey to Adelaide and then across the huge Nullarbor Desert and on to Kalgoorlie and Perth. He bought a small wagon to be pulled behind our car. On it, apart from our sleeping equipment, tents, and clothes, we carried spare tyres and large containers of water. We drove to Adelaide, a pretty city with "a pub on one corner and a Presbyterian church on the other." Elegant black swans decorated the ponds in the green spaces which were dotted everywhere. We went in search of our "Australian grandmother" – the little old woman whom Robyn had befriended on our sojourn to South Island, New Zealand. She was delighted to see us. Robyn hugged her, wanting her to come along with us across the Nullarbor.

This was going to be quite an adventure! Few Australians ever crossed the Nullarbor, especially by car, in 1962. Most of the way was marked by tracks in the loose sand made by huge Albion trucks with heavy loads. There were no actual roads, fewer outposts, and just endless stretches of sand with tired-looking bushes and ever-present sheep seeking non-existent pastures. Here, it took three acres to feed one sheep.

The greatest immediate problem was the "bulldust." Due to the fact that there was no delineated road, the way forward was in the path of the large trucks and semis that made their way through the desert. This posed its own set of problems. Our tyre width was much smaller. If we were to follow the tracks of these huge vehicles, then we had to be careful not to end up sitting on a bite of sand on our sump, with wheels spinning in the dust. There were huge potholes that were not immediately visible as we came upon them. The dust filled them in with fine sand to create an illusion of a stable surface. When we navigated into one of these, the car would slump and roll and the wheel would disappear into the hole, leaving our vehicle in a grotesque position. Trying to pull the car out would make the other wheels spin and get no traction but simply blow the bulldust in all directions like a sandstorm. We drove slowly and with great care and, some days, managed quite well. On others, we had to be rescued by trucks with built-in winches and helpful drivers.

Everything that was not nailed down was covered with a fine layer of red-brown sand. At the end of the day, my face was streaked with red where perspiration had made white channels on the sandy red surface. Even my teeth were gritty. We kept all the windows and the door tightly shut, but this was only marginally helpful; at the end of the day, when we stopped to pitch camp, piles of sand would fall from the doors to the ground, and everything inside was layered in red.

We stopped in this featureless plain near the Great Australian Bight and cast our tent for the night in between the sparse vegetation. We were exhausted, dirty, dishevelled, and glad to climb into our sleeping bags. During the night, we were awakened by the pad, pad, pad, noises of the tiny feet of creatures trying to examine our sleeping quarters. Out in the starlit night, under the southern constellations, were groups of curious black wallabies (a small species of black kangaroos) They were so cute and un-menacing that Robyn wanted to go and pat them. But they were wild and could pack a mighty punch when the occasion called for self-defence. After the first few nights, we accepted the kangaroos as part of the landscape and slept peacefully, despite all the hopping and padding around us in the night.

The one outstanding characteristic of the landscape was the sameness – day after day through the largest flat surface on earth, estimated at 77,000 square miles. Then, on our third day out, we entered a land of total desolation. There were no animals and no green plants except for saltbushes. It was like living on the moon.

We knew that we had to follow the truck paths, for if we strayed accidentally, we would be doomed. Driving was very tiring and, after a day or two, totally boring, but we slugged onwards. We had no option except to do what we had set out to do. Tom was terribly tired every evening. We were pushing hard to get to the halfway point, which was a small collection of buildings including a garage and the inevitable pub. This little outpost marked a milestone for us. We were salivating to get there and see a little settlement, no matter how small. Originally, this little outpost near the coast was manned by a radio–telegraph operator. What a lonely existence!

We were looking forward to the company of people and the luxury of a shower. There were artesian wells and their water was brackish, not really drinkable, but, at that point, I would give my kingdom for a shower to dislodge the sand from every crevice of my body! I brought along one precious bar of soap especially made for brackish water, as ordinary soaps will not lather in salty water. We headed for the bar and ordered deliciously long, cool drinks. Even Robyn was allowed in. He sat on a bar stool and enjoyed bottles of orange juice. We put on clean clothes and no longer itched; our skin began to regain its original hue. My scalp no longer shed red sand, and I was feeling hysterically happy.

We pitched our tent nearby and then were invited to join the happy festivities of this special night. It was the barmaid's birthday, certainly an excuse for celebration. People came in large trucks,

I have no idea from where, and joined in the celebrations as if we were all long-lost family. Robyn was the only child present, so the bar rules were suspended for him. He spent the night joining in the celebrations. We sang old English and Scottish songs and were constantly being introduced to more people as they arrived to join the party. Two very strange-looking rabbit catchers, their hats firmly glued to their heads, had corks twirling on strings from the brims and jiggling around their heads to keep the flies at bay. Someone took off to notify the local policeman (I have no idea where his outpost was located) so that the bar would not be fined for staying open after hours. It was about midnight when the local cop arrived and joined in the general merriment. This was, without doubt, the happiest party I had ever been invited to. We went home about midnight to our tent to rest our weary bones, as Robyn was looking tired and Tom was nearing the point of utter exhaustion.

We dragged on towards our goal the next day, but we felt clean and rejuvenated and ready to battle our way once more into the nothingness that was the Nullarbor. When we reached Kalgoorlie, we knew that we had almost made it. We got to a hotel and asked whether we could pay them to use not only their lawn to pitch our tent, but also their bathing facilities. They were most obliging, as very few private cars ever crossed the entire Nullarbor. That evening, the hotel owner came over and presented us with a certificate which informed all those who read it that we had, single-handedly, as a family, crossed the largest desert on Earth from one end to the other.

I still have memories of our great Australian adventure. Today, there is a train that carries passengers and freight across the Nullarbor, and the road has been levelled near the train track. We realized that we had the adventure of a lifetime in the "good old days."

WESTERN AUSTRALIA ODYSSEY

Tom rented a furnished house for us on Barnsley Road. Perth. For the better part of a year after our arrival, we packed and stored the camping gear in which we had lived for almost the entire year since our arrival in Australia. It felt strange to have a bedroom with a dressing table but nothing to put on it. Nevertheless, our priorities lay elsewhere.

Our very first act was to go out, find a breeder of Pekingese puppies, and buy one. Lulu, as we called her, was a tiny bundle of fur with a flat Chinese face and melting brown eyes, but with the annoying habit of being always underfoot. We had to be very careful not to step on her. We decided that there was to be a rule: no shoes were to be worn indoors.

Robyn hated to be in a room of his own and, feeling insecure in his new environment, would bring a pillow and a blanket to the foot of our bed. We would find him there during the night on the carpet.

Rob went to the local school, and I went to my job in the psychological services of the education department. For the first few days, I smuggled in Lulu in a cardboard box, shut the door to my office, and let her roam around and sleep under my desk while I made plans to see children at the school for the deaf. Lulu was so tiny that we felt badly about leaving her alone for any length of time, as she would cry pitifully and it would break all our resolve.

Tom started looking seriously for a "real" job. He went to see the people in Freemantle who worked for the same firm that had employed him in South Africa. Within half a day, he came home saying that he had been appointed by the London office as general manager of the Freemantle branch, which serviced Perth. He was relieved and ecstatic. We could now make plans.

I would come home after work and cook dinner for the three of us. Outside was a strategically placed clothesline, and on it were three Ozzie Kookaburras. These are large birds about a foot in height with beige-brown and greyish feathers. They would communicate with one another and also with me, trying to solicit food. Their cries were like the sound of old men laughing. They were positively hilarious. As I cooked, I laughed at their ribald laughter. Those birds made my day. They stayed on the clothesline all the time we lived in the house. When we moved, we missed them dreadfully.

We bought a piece of land in City Beach, on a rise about a block from the water, with fantastic views. We had spent some time looking for a plot of land and had had some interesting experiences with realtors. One, who had shown us a beautiful piece of land high on a hill overlooking the city, had, when we showed some interest, done us the favour of cutting down all the trees and indigenous vegetation – clearing the land to a flat and featureless block of sand "ready to build." We were appalled and told him so. "Bloody migrants!" he called us, as we refused to buy the disfigured landscape.

I designed our house, and an architect did the plans. But all did not go well. We had our ideas, and the Ozzies had theirs. I ordered jarrah for the window frames. This is a beautiful reddish gold wood that can withstand the elements. It comes from the Jarrah Forests from the southern part of Western Australia. I had specified that they were to be oiled and *not* painted. I arrived one afternoon after school to find the painter happily slapping brown oil paint on the frames. I asked him whether he had read the plans and said that, in any case, he would have to remove the paint or the frames, whichever he decided was best. He swore at me: "Bloody migrant! This is how we do it here." He continued to paint. I removed the paint can and asked him to leave the premises. "I only take orders from the builder," he said.

"So, why don't you go and ask the builder?" I quipped.

Then there was the matter of the wandoo flooring. This is a beautiful Australian hardwood. The main problem was that it was sold by the batch. Some batches had knots in them and could not be laid down as flooring. The pile of floorboards had to be ordered and then sorted by hand. Tom and I spent an entire weekend doing this backbreaking job.

On the following Wednesday, I stopped at the house to see how the job was coming along and found a carpenter laying the floorboards in neat rows from the pile of discarded boards. I went up to him and explained the problem. He ignored me and went on hammering the next board from the wrong pile. As far as he was concerned, I was just to be ignored. I phoned Tom and asked him to come as soon as he could. Within the hour, Tom arrived. I presumed that he would be able to sort things out man to man. The carpenter continued laying the boards. Tom approached gingerly and explained that they would have to come out. The carpenter ignored him, too, and continued hammering. It was as if we were not there at all!

This was one of the few times I ever saw Tom loose his cool. He approached the guy, pulled on his shirt collar, and made him stand up. "You will not listen to me, but who in hell do you think is paying your wages?" he asked the man, who was taken by surprise, backed away, threw down his hammer with force, and left in a huff.

The next day, we informed the builder that he had better do some supervision and that we were not paying wages to carpenters who refused to follow the plans.

The entire floor had to be removed and we had to start again, sorting more piles of suitable lumber.

My house was unusual, not like local houses at all. It was split-level and made entirely of the white brick I so admired. This brick, which resembles beach sand, never needs to be painted. I wanted a fireplace made of clinker brick in the living room. This is the brick which is fired over and over again in the kiln. These bricks become a rich red with purple distortions made by the fire. Some bricks have iridescent colourations, and some are a little uneven. I was laughed at! Nevertheless, I persevered and, for weeks, did the round of brick makers and bought discarded clinker bricks. We ended up with a glorious wall and a fireplace that would, against the white brick interior walls, have graced any architectural magazine.

Unlike Ozzie houses at the time, mine had a large walk-in closet in the bedroom. In those days, such a thing was unheard of, as every house had wardrobes in the bedrooms. We also had an en-suite bathroom in the master bedroom. But we ran out of money, so we laboriously tiled it ourselves. I also did the landscaping.

Building the garden was difficult, as the ground was beach sand. I researched the matter of the grass and found a coarse variety sustainable in this kind of soil. I hired a bulldozer and tried to get rid of the rocks and boulders in front of the house. The bulldozer owner had only one thing in mind – levelling everything. I told him my plans, but he promptly ignored them. I ordered him off the property unless he followed my instructions. He left. So much for Ozzie labourers! Friends helped us remove a large boulder. We planted the grass ourselves. It was labour-intensive, as we had to plant it by hand in tufts and rows. It took what seemed ages and was very exhausting work.

When we finally moved in, we were pleased with our efforts, except for the fact that we had a double-storey house instead of a single-storey one. The front section, built on the sand, had receded, leaving a large expanse under the house, all bricked in by the foundation. So, we had the builder cut in a door. We had a basement we had not planned for! Tom and some neighbours gave us a hand pulling out the sand from the interior. We ended up with a large, airy space we had not counted on. Still, after all our wanderings, we had a home at last.

Tom was enjoying his job. We made an effort to settle down and start a new life. I enjoyed my work and made friends. But things were not rosy in the garden. To my horror, I was being paid fifty-two dollars every two weeks. I thought that these were starvation wages, and I said so. Australian women were not in the habit of complaining.

My family and I went off to Rottnest Island for the weekend and returned on the ferry in the middle of a howling gale. We explored the countryside, revelling in the beautiful wild flowers unique to Western Australia. I loved my job but resented the fact that I was paid a fraction of the men's wages when I had better qualifications – and after I had sacrificed so many years to studying in the hopes of reaching a nirvana away from the turmoil of apartheid.

I enrolled in the local university and did a few courses, but my heart was not in it. Robyn was attending a great school: a Church of England private school. He revelled in his choir singing, and the school produced some ambitious productions. His writing and attitude both improved.

Then we had the news that Lena had finished school and was heading out to stay with the family. We were delighted. Robyn was particularly fond of his older sister and so was ecstatic when we told him that she was coming out to stay with us. She had passed her finals but had not made the grade into the university. For that, she needed to rewrite her botany exam. I was tailor-made to help her, so, with some studying and coaching, she finally sat for the final paper and passed.

We had not really had time to think of the fact that Western Australia was so far away from the rest of the inhabitants of this vast land. There really was nowhere to go travelling. It was thousands of miles just to get to the other cities. There were no cities or real developments north of Perth at that time, except for isolated outposts. The south, too, was only lightly populated and had little of interest. The city of Perth was pretty on the Swan River, but I was beginning to feel isolated and unhappy. I said nothing. I ploughed on. I joined the union to try and get better pay conditions, but the men's hostility was hurtful. I knew that the old traditions would prevail to keep professional women ever from attaining equal pay standing for equal qualifications. I was discouraged and demoralized.

DECISIONS, DECISIONS!

Meanwhile, I had been working in a job where I was in charge of assessing children with special needs. These included children of the school for the deaf, the school for children with muscular dystrophy (most of whom died at sixty years of age or thereabouts), hospital schools (generally for children in casts with hip dysplasia), and the Spastic Centre. I had my time cut out for me. I loved the job and felt that, as I had recently received information on the latest ideas in these areas while in South Africa, I was ahead of my colleagues in terms of repertoire of knowledge. I set to, with vim and vigour and loved every minute of my daily rounds.

My favourite venue was the school for muscular dystrophy, which is a dreadful hereditary disease. We often saw several children of the same family in the school. One group of Aboriginal siblings had five members in the school, all awaiting the same fate – a paralyzing death at about age sixteen. In the meanwhile, these children had to have the opportunity to grow up and learn about life in general and those things that would impact them in particular. They had the good fortune to have an ambitious, dedicated principal and, to say the least, a most insightful director who had transformed the school into one of the happiest places I have ever had the pleasure to visit. Although the children had their days numbered, their days were, while they lasted, just sheer, unmitigated *fun*.

There was joy in the little faces that surrounded me. Did I know that they were planning a trip around the world? They were going to leave shortly, as soon as they had got all the logistics arranged. There were quibbles about what size of ship to take on this fabulous journey. Then there was the route: deciding which route to take and what continents to visit. Then there was the problem of what to take on the voyage. Were potatoes really cheap in Chile? Then, of course, there was celestial navigation, which the older boys had to master. So much to do and so little time to straighten out all the wrinkles! Would I like to come along? They had been planning the trip for two years. What would I be able to contribute? One boy told me that as I was pretty and seemed to be fun, I should definitely plan to come along for the good times ahead. I was very touched, especially when I glanced at the late-stage fifteen-year-old children already incapacitated and in wheelchairs, awaiting a very different fate from the one they had planned. When the older boys deteriorated, they went into a special ward and were not in contact with their schoolmates. This way, the illusion of "all fun" could stand the test of time.

The Spastic Centre housed all those children who had neurological insults to the brain, generally due to asphyxiation at birth, which killed off the brain cells and which, in turn, affected the functioning of the arms, legs, and other body parts. There was no cure; there was merely adaptation.

The only "normal children" were those in the hospital school who had hip dysplasia. They were in hospital sometimes for two years, but their affliction did not impair their intellectual functioning. Therefore, to me, they were essentially "normal kids." Then there were the "accidents." These always left me feeling hollow and very sad. One small boy who was partially deaf was thrown against a wall by his irate father because he did not do what his father wanted and had to "learn the hard way"! His father ended up in jail, and the boy was so severely injured that he became partially paralyzed and was placed in an institution.

Another sad case was the one in which one of the "navvies" (dock workers) had undertaken to look after his newborn baby. The mother did not want the child and told him to take it if he wanted it. He did. But as he worked on the docks all day, he would leave the baby, well fed and well diapered, in his truck all day, only periodically changing and feeding the small child. At the age of a year, he was probably the most neglected child I had ever seen. His eyes showed no interest in anything. He was genetically normal but environmentally so unstimulated that he was mentally retarded. We removed him from his father's care and placed him in a home where he was massaged every three hours, as a means to try and stimulate him. We tried to introduce him to as many different experiences as we were able to conjure up, in an effort to provide some of the experiences that he had earlier missed.

* * *

We lurched along, but the final effort was worth it. It was a beautiful house, unlike any in the neighbourhood. It had a glorious view of the surf, and we were proud of The Ozzies do not like change. They are set in their ways and hate the idea that new "migrants "should have different ideas from those already set in stone. But the main problem, in my estimation, was that they had dreadful taste. "It is only in their mouth," Tom said in disgust. I agreed!

We were getting settled. Robyn was sent to an Anglican prep school of good repute and was having a blast singing in the choir. Lena finished school in South Africa after coming out to Oz for me to help her rewrite her failed science exam. She disliked the sexist attitudes of the boys she met and decided that she was going back to South Africa. She and a girlfriend rented and shared an apartment next to my mother's apartment. Mom kept an eagle eye on them. Tom had established himself at work as a senior executive at Neilson, the same Canadian firm that employed him originally in South Africa. He was stationed in Freemantle, just south of Perth.

I went on working for the psychological services. I loved the work, but I hated the system. I was probably the best-qualified person in the department, but I got the lowest salary because I was a *bloody woman!* I hated the sexist attitudes, but I realized that the Ozzie women were used to this system and were not motivated to remedy old ills. Most of the women were married, so they could depend on their husbands to bring home the bacon.

The only woman who was struggling was one whose husband had been killed in the war. She had no other source of income, despite having two small children to feed. I loved my job, but I knew that no matter what I did, I would always have to contend with the fact that I was constrained because of my gender. Unless I had a sex change, I would always be overworked and underpaid! Western Australia was not going to modify its ways any time soon, and especially not on my account!

There was to be a series of lectures on sleep disorders in children. It was up my alley. I wrote to the department and informed them that I was going to the lectures on the Friday and that I was going to leave work one hour earlier than usual. I was going to pay for the privilege. I could have gone anyway, but I thought it only right to let the department know my intentions. On the Monday, there was a note on my desk. I was going to have my salary cut because I was absent from work without permission! I was stunned. Devastated, I went home and cried. I had no future here. On the Monday, I wrote my letter of resignation. Tom told me to stay home and relax. I was broken-hearted and cried a lot. I had not done that in many years!

I recall that one of the single women in the department, one with a great sense of humour, had been looking at the new salary-scale postings. They were carefully annotated with "p.a." ("per annum"). After each column of figures, she looked searchingly. In the middle of lunch, she turned around and said in a loud but ostensibly innocent voice, for all to hear, "I never knew what the *p.a.* meant, but I guess I do now! Of course, it is the 'penis allowance'!"

THE ABO FROM SHARK BAY

He had arrived in Perth, Western Australia, on the morning plane, accompanied by the public health nurse. He was just five years old and very small for his age. He had a very black face, newly cut hair, and enormous black, pleading eyes. He was an Aboriginal from the northwest of the province of Western Australia.

His parents were, I was told, fence-menders; they were on permanent "walkabout," walking hundreds of miles and seeing to it that the property fences on a sheep station the size of a small country were kept in good repair. They took with them their entire family, comprising an older uncle and their five children of various ages. They walked vast distances in a forbidding landscape where there were no cities, no towns, and scarcely any other inhabitants except, perhaps, some other Abos also going on walkabout. A colleague of mine once remarked that he came from a place where there was no "there" there!

The little fellow's parents and extended family could survive only because of their intimate knowledge of this sparse land. The job suited them well, as they would have gone wandering about anyway in the course of living their normal lives.

The small child who had come from the plane, led by the hand by the district nurse, had a lost and woeful expression. He traded in a loincloth for the full regalia of a school uniform, replete with hard black lace-up shoes, untied shoelaces, long grey socks, grey pants, and a white shirt with a knotted tie. The ensemble was topped by a grey blazer, several sizes too big for his small frame, so that his hands kept disappearing into the sleeves. He had a perpetual runny nose and kept trying to wipe it on his sleeve, to the irritation of the nurse, who kept providing him with a handkerchief, which he looked at closely with an air of mystery.

He traipsed after the nurse, his shoes making a plopping sound and seeming not to coordinate with his arms hidden in the long blazer sleeves. I had made an arrangement to fetch him from the residential school for the deaf and bring him to the offices of the psychological services in order to make some assessment of his intellectual capacity and potential for learning language, and also to find out whether there might be some sign of neurological damage, such as aphasia. Tests at the Centre for the Deaf concluded that he had profound hearing loss; as such, it was unlikely that he would ever produce meaningful speech. We estimated that he was about five years of age. He had not been picked up at the age of two, specified by Australian law as the time when children with hearing loss had to be reported and assessed so that appropriate language stimulation may be provided by the department responsible for the education of the deaf.

The first night in Perth had, no doubt, been a revelation to him. The kindly nurse left him for the night in the dormitory of the residential school for the deaf. He had been fed strange food and then given a bath. When he was put to bed on a spring mattress and, horror of horrors, his caretakers tried to cover him with a sheet and blanket, he lay there crying softly. Then, when nobody was looking, he moved to the mat beside the bed and finally fell into the sleep of the utterly exhausted.

Early the next morning, he was wakened by the ear-piercing vibrations of the school bell. He hid under the bed. When the caretakers came to help him dress, he was nowhere to be found. The matron finally located him and dressed him, taking him into the rowdy breakfast hall, where the children were eating oatmeal topped with soft brown sugar and milk.

He was handed a spoon. He poked his finger into the hot cereal, making paths through it as if playing in sand. The school monitor pounced on this and started to shout, telling him that his manners were disgusting. He knew that something was wrong, but he could not figure out exactly what. The matron came over during the commotion and helped him to hold the spoon and eat his breakfast. He finally learnt how to get the now almost cold porridge into his mouth without spilling most of it on his spanking new uniform. It was a tricky manoeuvre for the uninitiated. He finally got the hang of it, only to find that the matron had to get a new pair of pants for him, as the first pair was irrevocably covered in oatmeal and sugar.

A strange bell rang; everyone scampered off. The boy tried to follow, but he had not the faintest idea where he was supposed to go. He needed to go to the toilet, so the matron took him to the boys' urinal. After she left him there, he had no idea how to undo the buttons of his trousers. The matron once again rescued him. He had tried to dribble a little through his pant leg, but it was a difficult thing to do, especially as he had to aim in the direction the matron had indicated. He did his best. But he was wet, uncomfortable, and ashamed.

The public health nurse took the boy to the audiometer lab, where he attempted to follow directions. But it was difficult, as he was profoundly deaf and the only sounds he was able to hear were in the basso profundo range. Because he had practically no residual hearing except in the very low frequencies, even with the most powerful hearing aids he would not be able to distinguish enough sound to learn meaningful language. He would need to learn sign language.

It is difficult, if not impossible, to test such a child and come to any real or meaningful determination of his potential. The tests available all have a cultural bias; as such, they have no validity for a deprived child living in an outback environment. Standardized tests are only valid for the population on whose performance they have been standardized. It was bad enough using tests standardized for American children on Australians.

I played with the boy using coloured blocks, but he did not seem interested in them. He picked them up, determined that they were not edible, and quickly lost interest. He looked pathetic and uncomfortable. He folded his legs in front of himself, put his chin on his knees, and looked as if he might burst into tears at any moment in this strange environment. I knew that whatever tests I tried with him would give only spurious results. I was at a loss. Whatever native intelligence he might have had was certainly locked away and inaccessible to me to assess in the depths of my cultural misunderstanding and amid his fear and alienation. I wanted to hug him, but I had no idea whether this gesture would further alienate him – or, perhaps, scare him to death.

The principal of the school for the deaf came in. He was a large, burly, red-faced man of Scottish ancestry with a marked Scottish accent and a no-nonsense attitude. I did not know him well, but I soon found out that he was like the proverbial bull in the china shop.

"Dinna worry, lass," he said. "He just needs whipping into shape."

I went back to my office, terribly concerned. How could I make recommendations for this little boy's placement? I did not have any valid tests that might have otherwise given me insights into his abilities. I had nothing available to me that would provide a framework for making decisions for the future of this small Aboriginal boy, whose whole life experience had been one of being with parents and siblings in the outback, and who, as far as we could determine, had never heard a single sound.

I was fighting the idea of placing him in the school for the deaf, where he would, no doubt, have been terrorized by the headmaster's "whipping him into shape." Australian law decreed that this was the way forward, however. Small children with profound hearing loss were placed into the school in order to give them an opportunity for stimulation and speech development.

I was not, in all conscience, able to make the kind of recommendations required. I was totally against the idea of incarcerating this little waif in a system that would traumatize him emotionally, cut him off from his family and siblings, and achieve negligible gains in the area of socialization. His culture taught him other things – things that would be relevant in his daily life in the bush. All the schooling in the world would not give him this. The "whipping into shape" promised by the headmaster might destroy him. I could not be a party to this.

Then there was the fact that if he stayed in school, he would likely be rejected by his peers, which would be a painful and useless lesson. If and when he returned to his parents, he would feel a stranger who had forgotten his family ties. Acceptance by his siblings, wise in the ways of the bush, would be difficult.

His fate would probably be to ultimately resume his place with his parents on walkabout, no matter what education he received. They loved him and found his handicap merely a nuisance in their daily routines. He would probably get employment with the farmer who paid his entire family for the fence-mending. His life, like that of his parents, would be rich with emotional connections and gainful employment. He would be accepted by the other members of the tribe and stood a good chance of being happy despite his severe disability.

I spent an entire day mulling things over. It was not in my power to make the final decision. I was there only to advise and to uphold the law. I knew that I would get no support from the principal, who seemed to be imbued with tunnel vision, and no sympathy for the Aboriginals, whom he regarded as aberrant and ignorant.

I sought out the public nurse. She appeared to be a woman of vast experience and, I suspected, a sympathetic point of view. I asked her to meet me for lunch. We talked of this and that, and I finally broached the subject of the Abo from Shark Bay. I told her of my difficulties and concerns. I also found out that the boy's parents were in Shark Bay awaiting news of their son. They came into town only twice a year to collect their stipend. They appeared, from all accounts, to be a happy family. The older boys, who were of the age to leave their parents, continued to stay with them and mend fences. They were happy with their lot in life.

I thought that it was time I voiced my doubts. Suddenly, the nurse got up and gave me a hug. She had had the same concerns, but she, too, had to follow the rules, which included taking the boy to Perth for the assessment. We spent the afternoon colluding to defy the law. She was going to send the boy back to his parents. It was the only humane thing to do. She would, out of her own pocket, buy a return ticket on a flight and take him home. I would help in every way I could.

The public nurse whisked the boy away from the school the next morning. I had managed to get him clothes that did not specify that he was student at the school for the deaf. The first thing we did was discard his shoes and socks. He grinned for the first time since he had arrived in Perth.

The nurse often took small commuter planes back to her base, so she called on a pilot she knew for help. He agreed that *mum* was the operative word. The last I saw of the boy was when he got into the plane, hanging on for dear life to the nurse's hand.

I knew that I would be walking a fine line, too. The assessment notes I had made, which were to be given to the office for typing, mysteriously disappeared. I was also in possession of the optometry assessment. That, too, went the way of my report.

I spent about a month terrified that I might be found out and that the principal would call me on the progress of the boy from Shark Bay. Then, a very fortuitous thing happened. The principal was transferred to another school. For a year, I had avoided him like the plague. He was the only one who could call my bluff in this instance.

I received a postcard from the nurse. She thanked me for my help and reported that the "parcel" had been delivered safely. I was so relieved.

Profound deafness creates so much social isolation even in the most receptive of environments, and even in the presence of a loving family, such as was the case for the Abo boy. I was absolutely sure that the incarceration of that small, vulnerable child who was obviously well and happy in his outback walkabout environment and in the loving bosom of his family would have had disastrous consequences for his future happiness.

It was a year later that I decided to leave Australia. I had many personal reasons for leaving. I have never forgotten the episode of the Abo from Shark Bay.

RESOLUTIONS AND FRESH BEGINNINGS

It seemed to me almost counterproductive to think of leaving Australia. We had sampled the climate of most of the provinces and had even crossed the Nullarbor. We had ploughed through the good, the bad, and the ugly. We liked most of it and had even begun to feel at home. We had invested time and effort in our explorations, and most of our money in "settling down" in Perth. We loved our new house, having struggled long and hard not only to have it built, but also to ensure that it was something that we thought reflected our taste and hard work.

Now the dream was crumbling. I knew with startling clarity that no matter what I did in this beautiful little corner of the world, none of my past sacrifices in the areas of study and work were ever going to bear fruit. I was irrevocably and indisputably the wrong gender, and nothing was going to change that. I was going to get a "woman's" pay for the rest of my life. All my long years of study meant absolutely nothing in comparison to being the "wrong" gender!

I went into a kind of depression. I wanted to roll up in a ball and just fade away. I did not want to communicate or laugh at anything anymore. Joy had gone out of life. I, who had had a rather philosophical attitude to life, just did not want to try anything anymore. I did not want to go anywhere. I did not want to do anything. I would curl up and stare at walls.

I did not even want to cook. Tom came home and did chores and also produced dinner. He was getting worried about me, but any of his words of encouragement fell on deaf ears. I slouched and pined away my days. Then Tom hit on an idea. "Why do you not catch a boat and go to Canada and see what it has to offer?" he suggested. At first, I did not think it was a serious proposition. Soon after, however, Tom bought me a ticket. I said goodbye to the family and to Western Australia, caught a ship that sailed to Sydney, and then travelled, via Japan and Hawaii, into Vancouver, British Columbia.

I shared a berth with three vibrant young Ozzie girls who shook me out of the doldrums and took me with them on an exploration of Japan. We caught a bullet train to rejoin the ship on its way to Hawaii and Southern California. I finally disembarked in Vancouver on one cloudy morning while I was in the middle of a severe migraine headache. I promptly caught a taxi in the drizzle and asked to be taken to the "nearest school district headquarters."

"The nearest is on Tenth Avenue," said the driver. I made my groggy way to the main office counter in the school district headquarters.

I asked whether there were any positions available. "That depends," said the secretary. "What can you do?" she asked.

"Well, a few things," I replied. "I like to teach young children!" She shuffled the papers and ask me to fill in a questionnaire. I sat on a hard wooden school bench and filled in the paperwork. I was feeling nauseous. I turned the papers in and prepared to leave, but as I got to the outer door, I heard a shriek. "Come back! Come back!" the secretary shouted. "Why did you not tell me you are *school psychologist*?"

"You did not ask," I replied.

"Do you know that we have sixteen vacancies that we cannot fill?" I was very surprised. She explained that it was not that child psychologists were hard to find, but it was that all school psychologists in Canada had to also be registered teachers. (This is not so in the States.) "Can we arrange to give you an interview with someone now?" I was beginning to revive. It is so nice to be wanted!

Minutes later, she had found "someone in the building" – an elderly gentleman who was in the process of retiring and who, during our short conversation, elaborated at length on the trials and tribulations of being a diabetic. After sharing some more confidences, he got up. As I reached the door, he said quite seriously, "By the way, what does a school psychologist actually do?"

"More things than I could possibly mention," I replied. I wished him well and went down to the secretary to say goodbye.

"Give me five minutes before you go. By the way, you're hired! Start in September!" she said. I was groggy, overjoyed, and in disbelief. In fact, even my migraine felt better! I promised to phone in with my new address. I flew in a taxi back to the boat to retrieve my luggage from customs and then tried to get some local accommodation.

I had only one criterion: I wanted to be near the sea. Within half an hour, I found a miniscule bachelor's apartment a block from the sea at English Bay. I took it right away when I saw the price and the sea view. I was home. I slept in my sleeping bag on the floor. The next day, the super told me that there was a tenant leaving and wanting to dispose of a double bed. I asked him whether he could get it to my apartment. I paid him in cash for his efforts (fifty dollars, as I recall). I was brimming with excitement. My new life, pregnant with possibilities, had begun. I phoned Tom with the news, counting my meagre pennies in a phone booth. He was pleased as punch and proud of me.

I did not want to think far ahead, but I remembered that Tom had left Canada aeons ago with the firm resolve not to return – ever! He had survived the Great Depression in North Battleford, Saskatchewan, and the Canadian military as a captain stationed in Alaska (sometimes in heavy-duty vehicle trials that were conducted in minus –85° Celsius weather). He wanted to see the world, and that he did. Under no circumstances did he ever want to come back. His memories of the loss of his family (when they had all gone back to England after losing their farm during the Depression) were still fresh in his heart. He had faced the world alone and had survived. How could I even suggest that he return?

I did not broach the subject. I just went about my daily life and did not consider tomorrow. It was early days yet, and there were many variables to consider. Time was on my side.

ADJUSTING TO CANADIAN WAYS

I was posted to an elementary school and to a "special class." When school started in September, I went to the staff meetings and met my colleagues. I was aching to get going. My new colleagues were very friendly, but they looked at me askance, as if I was out of my mind to teach the special class. This did not spoil my resolve. I had been in special classes many times before and knew that the children would be a challenge, but that was what made it so interesting!

There were only seven children, all fitting different pathology labels and all needing to be taught to acclimatize to the classroom in order to learn useful life skills. Four of the children were hyperactive, the kind who long to hang onto the picture rails by their teeth! One of these was also partially deaf. They all had serious adjustment problems. They all came into the class with bravado, as if they had spent their days planning to outwit the system. I was only the latest manifestation of the order.

The first order of business was to get them allocated to special seats in the classroom (not for me were the nice little neat rows of a regular classroom). The object was to keep them as far apart as the room allowed. They needed space so that if things went awry (as they generally did), the children would impinge as little as possible on each other's territory.

Thomas came in with bluster. He took the seat nearest to my desk and informed me that he did not "do reading"!

"Well, you are in luck! We do not do reading in this classroom!" He went home and told his dad that he had found "the best teacher," who did not "do reading." The following afternoon, his dad appeared after class and asked me to explain myself. I invited him to join the class the next day. I placed a large armchair at the rear of the classroom, deciding to send notices to all the parents telling them that if they heard alarming tales, then they should feel free to join the class, sit in the special chair at the back, and take in the proceedings.

The next day, we started with math. I had what might be called a child's roulette wheel. All the students were all given chips. When the game started, they had to take a turn and tell me how many chips they had in total when they added the last count to their winnings. If they could not tell me how much it was, then they lost the chips. There was total silence and deep concentration. "I have twenty-two and now eight more, so I now have, um, thirty. Good I can keep the winnings!"

This was serious business, but I was also on the floor watching the proceedings in earnest. We had an open-door policy. A little later in the month, a small man came in, gingerly opened and closed the door, retreated to the parents' chair, and said nothing. I presumed that he was a parent. Class went on with the students' screams of delight over the "winnings." Later, the gentleman left. It was only later that day that I was told that an inspector from the school board had been there to see what I was up to.

Thomas's dad arrived and was in the parents' chair. I had not seen him arrive, but there he was, seeing Thomas "tell" me what was on a series of flash cards. If Thomas got it right, then he kept the card. He now had twenty-seven in his cache. But this was not reading! Within three weeks, Thomas had all the flash cards of *The Big Book of Pirates*. Then one afternoon, I suggested that as a special treat for Dad, Thomas might like to try the reader. "No," he said. "I can't read!" But I produced the book anyway, and he read well, recognizing all the flash-card words in the "dreaded book." He was proud as punch …

But Thomas had another problem. He had a brother in the school who was one year older and did not have perceptual problems. The two were in fierce competition. I connived with his brother's teacher and taught Thomas how to do a transaction in math (I think it was long division) which the brother's teacher had not yet taught her class. I sent up Thomas so he could "show the class" and, incidentally, his brother how to do long division. He was proud as he could be, and I suggested that he join the senior class to help the other children and show them how to do it. My aim was to boost this child who had a very poor self-image. Suddenly, he was a star. He still came to visit and do reading with me, and we finished *The Book of Pirates* series. Thomas had a superior IQ but very poor visual perception, and I understood from his mother that it was possible that he had had some brain injury at birth, which accounted for these anomalies. We moved him, with his newfound self-esteem, out and into a regular classroom. I understood that he continued to prosper.

There seemed to me to be a great deal of pushing and shoving among my students, so every morning, we started the foot circle. We sat in a circle, took off our shoes, and put our feet in a centre point. Nobody was allowed to speak, but each student had to tell another in the circle, using only the toes, that he or she liked that person. My class seemed to take this act seriously. My objective was to get them to think before engaging in the usual pounding of a smaller classmate.

Then there was the day when I told the class a "big secret": the following day was to be Chopper Day. I did not elaborate. One mum, horrified, phoned me. I explained things to her and set her fears to rest. The children would be given a big number (big numbers are much more powerful and exciting than smaller ones!), e.g. 98,398,273,618, divided by a number with zeroes (for example, 1,000,000), and the magic answer appeared by using the chopper to chop off the numbers corresponding to the number of zeroes. We drew large choppers and had pages of puzzles, and the students soon got the gist. Some later told me that they had shown their mums how to do it, for it was magic …

I always had boys in my classes. They are generally not as well developed as girls of the same age. I did have one small girl in the group. She sat at my desk. I did not want the boys to bully her, so I kept her under my wing. She not only was brain-damaged but also had a fairly low IQ.

She arrived every day dressed immaculately in frilly pink dresses and little pink slippers to match. She had many perceptual problems. Teaching her to read would take a couple of years, at least.

One snowy day, she suddenly got out of her desk and dashed to the door. "Catch me," she cried, opening the door and then dashing at great speed out of the school grounds and into an extremely busy street. I chased her, running as fast as I could, but she had had a head start and was threatening to cross the road, all the time turning to taunt me, without any regard to the traffic. I was terrified, but I finally caught her and dragged her back to school. I was very cross. "Catch me," as the definitive fun game to play with Dad, had to go! I asked her dad to come and visit. When he did, I explained the difficulties I had with this game! He promised to discourage it in future.

The most rewarding technique for eliminating tantrums was to completely ignore them and, in the meanwhile, go around the class nonchalantly and reward the other children with raisins for not paying attention to the tantrum. The child throwing the tantrum got no reward of attention and was encouraged by the class to "please continue" whenever he or she stopped; otherwise, no raisins!

I was accosted by the principal one morning. "You never come to my staff meetings," he said accusingly! "You must attend the next one." I told him that I could not leave the class alone. "I will remedy that," he said. "I will send you four grade-seven boys. They will do the job. You need not worry!" I went to the staff meeting with great trepidation. The grade-seven boys went into my classroom. Within ten minutes, there were frantic phone calls. One grade-seven boy nearly lost his ear after it was sliced by a garden tool; it was bleeding profusely. One child had climbed up to the top of the book cupboard and refused to come down. Another child had left the room and was "lost." We rushed back. There was blood everywhere from one boy's ear. The book cupboard had separated from the wall to which it had been fixed and was swaying precariously with a child on the top.

"I guess you will not be attending anymore staff meetings!" said the principal.

I was asked the following year to do "workshops" for teachers. About twenty teachers at a time were liberated from their classes, and I was to give them workshops on behaviour modification techniques and new teaching methodologies for brain-injured students. I had a wonderful year interacting with the teachers. The following year, I was moved into the Point Grey School District and started to work with a wonderfully enlightened school principal. I was the designated "area psychologist," but I refused to work with teens. It is imperative that psychologists have some insight into the culture. I was a new arrival and, as such, could not make assumptions about a culture to which I was so recently an arrival. Elementary schools were more appropriate workplaces for me.

Point Grey Elementary was a large school with six classrooms set aside for the yearly "intake" of new grade-one students.

The principal had a problem. He needed to decide where to place each new child, and he also needed to decide the methods by which the teacher would teach each new group of students. Previously, the parents were given the choice. This year, we decided to make the choices more scientific and to screen each child on a number of variables so that the teaching techniques would be appropriate for each child's learning style and developmental stage. This had never been done in Canada previously.

We first asked the teachers what methodologies they preferred to teach in their classrooms, and then we set up six different ways to teach reading: look-and-say, phonics, and so forth (the last class was a pre-reading class for those not yet developmentally ready to read). Then, we got the teachers onboard and started to look at the intake group.

I tested the girls first. It was a process of elimination. I knew that three-quarters of the girls would be ready to learn to read, as they were more perceptually mature. They would learn to read wherever we placed them. I picked out ten who needed special placement and decided to test them further, later on. Then I started on the boys.

We ushered in all the boys in rows and then asked them to walk a balance beam. Some went gingerly and made it to the end, but others fell off the beam constantly and could not seem to keep their feet and body in alignment. I made secret notes on their difficulties. Then there was the "draw a man" contest, which traditionally provided a good measure of a child's ability and visual perception, in relation to chronological age and sex. The little girls generally drew two circles (head and body), some arms, and stick legs, but then drew other embellishments such as hats, flowers, long skirts, dogs on leads, shoes with high heels, etc. Boys, on the other hand, drew one small circle (head), one slightly larger circle (body), two stick legs, and, quite often, a belly button. The "men' were never dressed but were often given a large belly button as ornamentation. (Freudian psychologists often argue that the belly button is, in fact, a displaced penis. The boys realized that doing this could be construed as "naughty" and unacceptable in polite society! So, belly buttons were offered in the stead of penises!)

Then there were squares and diamonds. Everyone (except the mentally retarded) could make a square, but the definitive test was the four-sided diamond shape (a point at the top and one at the bottom). Many six-year-old boys could not, for the life of them, duplicate the diamond shape. They could see the points but could distinguish how they went together. This was quite a definitive test of the maturity of visual perception. Without passing these obstacles, a child was probably going to have difficulties in learning to read and need more "maturational" time in order to succeed at visually distinguishing the shapes of letters of the alphabet.

Most children would mature enough during the first year in grade one to learn to read fairly rapidly, but there were always those with visual-perceptual difficulties who were in need of other methods if they were to learn to read (feeling the letters is one method; phonics, another). Many of the children could go into any class and learn to read. But about 20 per cent needed specific reading methods in order to mature and to guarantee that they did not start school life feeling that they could not "succeed." Two of the children were, I suspected, brain-injured and did not have the necessary equipment to learn to read in the first year. I contacted the parents, and both gave me details of difficult births where the mothers were in labour for some time and the doctors had difficulties establishing breathing in the babies they delivered. I suspected some brain injury under these circumstances.

Finally, we had segregated only those children who were not ready to read and put them in a class where the teacher could help them mature without making demands that they were not yet ready to meet. We looked at all the results and asked the teachers to decide what methods they preferred to teach. Subsequently, we moved the children to the appropriate classrooms. It is imperative to allow children to feel emotionally successful!

I collected all the children's draw-a-man contests and diamonds, and tracked their ability to "do" the balance beam. I tacked the results to the blackboard in one of the classrooms. Then the parents were invited to come and see the results and then discuss which class would best suit the needs of their child. I was lucky in that the parents were quite often themselves professors at the University of British Columbia, so I was able to expound on theories and know that I would probably be understood. I also assured the parents that these were normal variations in a population and that they did not reflect in any way that the child had a low IQ. What we were trying to achieve was to get the best initial fit, so as to prevent children from feeling that somehow they had "failed" reading!

These tactics could never be undertaken in a school with only one grade-one class, but as we had an embarrassment of riches in the form of six grade-one classes, it was possible to make reading rewarding from the start. This also provided some insight into the difficulties that grade-one teachers faced in the first years of school. If there was only one classroom, as in rural schools, then the teacher had to be all things to all children.

Teaching reading to English-speaking children is tricky at best, all over the English-speaking world! Latinos have an easier tack. A totally phonetic language is a breeze to teach! Latino teachers wonder what the fuss is about in schools that teach English-speaking children. They often only admit children aged seven into reading classes. (They do not then have to deal with those children who are naturally immature.) Americans resolved the issue with the Head Start Program. Younger (and often socially deprived) children were given programmes to ensure their exposure to formal language and a wide variety of visually stimulating objects, thereby ensuring that they would not fall behind in comparison to less-deprived middle-class children. It is a shame that some of these programmes were discontinued in many schools and are not universally available.

I never undertook this kind of work again, although I did keep an eye on the school. I must report that the teachers were very happy – and the parents even happier – with the results. These had been ideal situations, ones not often replicated in schools.

I then tested children and provided insights and advise for teachers about children who had been named as having "problems." I started working on partially deaf children (my special interest). All those children who had been referred as brain-injured at birth were of special interest. My secretary at the school board complained about the length of the reports and the recommendations offered.

I also was amazed at the head of the psychology department. He was of the old school, but he told me that all I had to do was record a child's IQ, as nothing else mattered. I was aghast! I was beginning to get discouraged. I gave workshops on the brain-injured child, of which there are many, undetected, in regular classrooms.

My work was different every day, and I so enjoyed working with special-needs teachers – we were comrades-in-arms! My cutting-edge knowledge was finally being put to good use!

*   *   *

Christmas was on the horizon. I had decisions to make. I had promised Tom that I would fly home for the Christmas holiday. I wanted to see my son, Robyn, and attend his choral society gala at the Anglican church. We had much to talk about.

Tom was still reluctant to come back to the country that had afforded him so much hardship in the past. He continued to joke and say that he knew what Canada could offer. "One could always starve to death," he would joke (as he had almost done in his youth during the Depression on the prairies). The alternative was that, as he said, "One could always freeze to death," as he had almost done in Alaska on manoeuvres with the Americans during the war.

After all, Tom was settled in a great job, Robyn was going to a wonderful school, and we had a nice house at City Beach. Why would I not just come back and be content?

His concerns were well founded, for I knew that I would never be happy being a housewife and staying home to bake pies. I had sweated and strained to go through seven years at university. I needed more in life. I had been given free rein in Canada, in terms of my job. I had had an interview in which it was proposed that I go to Langara College and set up a programme to teach techniques to use with brain-injured children and help teachers' assistants deal with behaviour modification in the classroom. Would I like to set up a new curriculum? It was all too good to miss. To top it all, I was given a fairly decent salary for the first time in my entire life!

I knew I was going to come back to Canada. Over Christmas 1968, I made the decision to return. Tom dragged his feet. Rob wanted to go with me when I went back to Canada, but I felt that he needed to stay in school and then come out with his dad at the end of the school year.

We arranged that Tom and Rob should stay and then be rewarded with a wonderful ocean voyage, during which they would visit the Orient, Honolulu, and Los Angeles and finally find their way to Vancouver. Robyn, mollified, subsequently made a scrapbook of his travels.

I met Tom and Rob in the Port of Vancouver on a wet, chilly morning. We all went back to my miniscule apartment in the West End. From there, we took an apartment in North Vancouver. I think that Tom was quite surprised at how much Canada had grown in his absence and how "civilized" it was! Our new life had finally begun!

SOUTH TO SINGAPORE

I have not spoken of the interesting life I had in Canada and abroad, as far as my career was concerned. I was appointed as programme coordinator to Langara College, and I taught a programme that had at its core a methodology for schoolteachers and classroom assistants to use in dealing with children who had neurological disorders. This programme elucidated learning disabilities in particular and showed how to deal with these in the classroom setting. It was the only programme like it in Canada at the time, although it was subsequently copied meticulously by several other colleges in British Columbia and in the United States. Then, after a visit from a teacher from the department of education in Singapore, I was asked to go Singapore in person and set up the programme there. There were major difficulties, as the university had no books on the subject at the time. Langara allowed me to take the books on the plane and lend them temporarily to the library in Singapore so that the students could have pertinent reference materials!

I was overwhelmed by the fact that when I gave my first lecture in Singapore, it took place in a cavernous hall with seating stretching to the back ceiling. Three hundred people were in attendance. I can only assume that most of the attendees were from other faculties and that they had assembled to hear of a subject about which there was not a great deal of information in those days and about which there seemed to be a great deal of curiosity. I have a suspicion that they wanted to see what Canadians had to offer. I was later told that they had started with the tried-and-true English, followed by the Australians and, in desperation, the Americans, and that they had all proved thoroughly disappointing. I felt constrained to shine for the Canadians, and I think I did!

I rented a small apartment near the college and ate out twice a day. One of my meals was supplied by hawkers who would come to the university grounds and cook delicious meals from barrels and carts that they brought in each day. I suspect that nobody eats at home in Singapore. Everywhere are large, cavernous marketplaces lined with hawkers' stalls offering everything from soup to nuts. After choosing a table, I made the rounds of all the stalls, gave my order (one plate to be freshly made and delivered to table 66, as an example), and then wended my way to the desserts and, finally, the fresh tropical fruit juices, placing my order for table 66. In a short time, the food arrived at the table, which, by that time, was probably being occupied by several locals, all expectantly awaiting their orders. The food was placed in a circular lazy Susan in the centre of the table, and then everyone, including those who had not received their orders, felt free to help themselves to some of the food I had ordered. By the same token, when someone else's food arrived, I was encouraged to take a sample. It was the friendliest table arrangements I had ever encountered. Ah, to have the same arrangements at home! I do see the problems, as this type of alfresco dining would never take hold in the frigid temperatures of a Canadian winter …

*   *   *

The schools in Singapore are most unusual in that they have to cater to the four different ethnic groups living locally – which is a nightmarish feat. English is the lingua franca, but there are Malaysians, Tamils from India, and a large Singaporean Chinese presence. The largest group was of Chinese Singaporeans, but therein lies a tale. When the English took over Singapore in the early days of empire and, more recently, after the war, the population was Malay. Then, Chinese people started immigrating to the peninsula. As there were no Chinese women available (since Chinese women stayed home in China and never ventured out alone), the men had, over time, married the Malay women. Hence the Singaporean Chinese are essentially all part Malay. Every child is catered to in a separate school, with separate teaching goals and different religions, and it is only when students reach the end of primary education that they switch to the lingua franca. High school students are all taught in English; otherwise, it would have been a nightmare! It is, however, a nightmare for mixed lower grades, which have not only different problems, but often children placed in the same class from different ethnicities, all trying to communicate but not having a common home language to speak at school! I admired their resourcefulness. Nevertheless, the linguistic and cultural complications were almost insurmountable! The primary reader was the same in all first grades, but the content was in one of four languages, including English. The private schools were taught only in English and were predominately filled with Caucasian students, all neatly attired in English school uniforms, blazers, and woollen knee socks! This in a tropical climate where the sun could melt pavements!

I managed to sublet a rather mangy apartment replete with lizards parading on the ceiling. These accompanied the cockroaches that came undisturbed and bold as brass out of the pipes in the bath and then spent all their time trying to escape from the steep sides of the bath itself, finally exhausting themselves and dying in the bottom of the bath. I only allowed myself to take showers; otherwise, I would have spent most of the time just disinfecting the bath. I had dreadful, soul-destroying furniture, so I bought some beautiful batik cottons and spent my time wrapping them onto the furniture with big hidden safety pins. I went to the gardener and contracted with him to rent some potted plants that he kept in a garden shed. He grew hysterical with laughter when I informed him that I would not buy the plants but just rent them, as I was flying home quite shortly. The horrible apartment turned into one that people enter and ask whether I had had a decorator come in!

Many of my spare moments were spent in the schools for the deaf. Here, the teaching was dysfunctional and the children's neurological problems were not understood. I noted that many of the students were drawn by the staff members of schools for the deaf, and I was pleased.

My days were extraordinary, my colleagues were more than generous, and the courses seemed to swell with attendees. Word was out that my lectures were terribly interesting and cutting edge; as a result, I seemed to have huge classes, but only about half of the attendees were, in fact, my registered students. I visited many schools and saw many children with dreadful problems who could have done well had the Singaporeans the necessary knowledge to help them. One case stands out. One poor little mite was born blind to a Chinese couple. They both worked, so they had solved the problem by strapping the child into a bed so he would remain safe till their return, at which time they would take him out of the bed and feed him. They could not comprehend that they had, in fact, produced a severely under-stimulated child who, by their actions, was guaranteed to be borderline mentally defective. I also saw a fifteen-year-old spastic girl who spent her life in an elevated wheeled bed. She was severely brain-injured at birth and spent her life strapped in so that she would not fall off her wheeled bed. When I engaged her, she trembled, threw her limbs about in spastic movements, and nearly fell out of the bed. I do not know why I decided to examine her. Some spark caught my attention. I tested her with a series of pictures telling a story about a dog who always did the wrong thing and suffered the consequences. She laughed at the jokes. This told me that, under all that pathology, she retained a remnant of intelligence. She had been labelled mentally defective. I set up a look-and-say reading programme for her. She was so excited that she was ecstatic, nearly falling out of the raised bed when she tried to thank me. She was going to finally learn to read at the ripe old age of sixteen! But more to the point, her life had been changed forever, and I was pleased. I saw her before I came home, and she was all smiles and surrounded by books displayed on a tablet. Singaporeans were indeed lagging behind other cultures in this modern world and had realised that they needed to make up for lost time. Just before I departed on the plane back to Canada, the faculty sent me a beautiful hand-embroidered jacket and the largest bouquet of exotic tropical blooms that I had ever seen as a "thank-you token".

But my lectures ignited the spark. Singaporeans at least realized that more had to be done. They made concerted efforts to upgrade their schools and bring them into the new century! I embarked and had endless problems trying to get my gifts on the plane to go home, in addition to all the crates of books I was bringing back to Langara after loaning them to the Singaporean library. The crates burst open on arrival, scattering the books around the customs shed!

As an aside, it dawned on me, over time, what an enormous contribution the South African Witwatersrand University had made to my life. It had given me cutting-edge knowledge from the start. I was often surprised by the fact that the information I had learned there was as good as, if not better than, that provided in more "advanced" countries (including the United States!).

FAMILY PROBLEMS

I had been happily living in Canada for several years, when I received an alarming phone call from my daughter. After several years in Europe, where her husband had been attending the Imperial College in London (and accumulating several degrees), she and her family finally returned to the Portuguese province of Mozambique with the intention of making it their home. I had thought that it was a terrible idea. Africa was in a phase of turmoil, of shifting sands and allegiances – and probable civil war. But my daughter had been given a house in Maputo. All she wanted was to settle down and bring up her two boys. I held my peace and made no comment on her decision.

Suddenly, one afternoon, I got a phone call telling me that Maputo (the newly named capital of Mozambique) was on the verge of anarchy. Things did not look good. What terrified Lena was the fact that she had actually heard gunfire. All her plans for a peaceful life had flown out the window, and she asked me whether I could help get her out of Mozambique and into Canada at the earliest possible opportunity. She had applied to come to Canada but found that the Canadian consulate was closed and that any interaction with the consulate had to be through Nairobi. Then came the news that the Nairobi consulate had also closed, and Lena felt stranded. All her paperwork and applications had disappeared overnight, and things were looking more and more unstable.

Could I take up the cudgels, so to speak, and see what I could do my end? I had no idea how to proceed, so I cast about and finally was told by colleagues at Langara College that perhaps I would have better luck if I approached my member of the Legislative Assembly. I did this and found that I got a great deal of attention. Things began to move.

All the Canadian consulates which normally looked after new immigrants were automatically closed in periods of strife. The only way to start the paperwork, I was secretly informed, was for the family to fly to Lisbon and go to the consulate there. In a matter of days, Lena flew with the children to Lisbon, abandoning all her possessions in the war-struck country. In Lisbon, she was able to disclose all the pertinent information about her family's being presently in Vancouver. She said that Tom was a war vet who was born in North Battleford and that, of course, I was not only a Canadian citizen but also a university professor with sufficient financial resources to support the family when they arrived. I posted a bond and accepted the responsibility of supporting the family when they came. In Lisbon, my grandchildren were officially de-wormed (I am not sure what that

148

entailed), given the necessary shots and vaccinations, and, within three weeks, were on their way to Vancouver, BC.

I went to pick them up at the airport. While I waited, I saw a lovely little boy standing next to one of the airport columns. I had never met him but knew instantly that the little one was my grandchild! He was a little disconcerted when a strange woman picked him up and kissed him.

I had purchased a rather commodious town house in Caufeild, in West Vancouver, at the time, so there was enough room for all of us, despite the fact that the children had to sleep in my sewing room. We managed.

During this period, my son-in-law decided to remain in Lourenco Marques and complete his academic year of teaching at the university. It was almost a year later when we drove to Seattle and picked him up. He had completed his contract and walked across the border into South Africa. From there, he flew to Canada.

By then, I had put down a deposit on a three-bedroom townhouse in North Vancouver, furnishing it with scraps from here and there. It was not elegant, but it was functional. I had spoken to my Son-in-law over the phone to consult him on the feasibility of the purchase. He agreed that it would be a great idea, as my house would have been too crowded with all of us in it.

So it was that when Rui, my son-in-law, arrived off the plane in Seattle and was processed at the customs office in Blaine, he could be driven to his own (sparsely furnished) house. During that period, I bought an apartment on the Ala Wai Canal in Waikiki, Hawaii. I would bundle up all the family and give them the keys to the house as well as airplane tickets to Honolulu for a family vacation. I would sometimes take the grandsons with me to Honolulu on month-long vacations, during which time they learnt to do Chinese calligraphy from a professional just for fun. They also learnt all about the joys of investing in their own "stock market." They had paper money. They bought stocks and watched them rise or fall on a daily basis. They could not get home fast enough from the beach to find out whether their particular purchases had gone up or down and whether their wealth had increased in the transaction. They had a great deal of fun – and may even have learnt something along the way.

Soon, my older grandson Ze was in school and the family was settled. Rui looked for a job. He was too highly qualified, he was told. But he had to put food on the table, so he got a job organizing a factory. It kept food on the table until he managed to get a more interesting job in his field. The family moved into a larger townhouse, and the children were both in school. My daughter was at a loose end, so we all suggested that she take the opportunity to enrol in a programme at Capilano University. After all, she lived almost opposite the grounds of the college. She fought tooth and nail *not* to go, but she finally enrolled in a course in looking after small children, which seemed appropriate. When she finally graduated and we held a small celebration for her, she told me how much she had resented having to study! She had always been the anomaly in a family where every member was highly educated, and wanted to hide behind the fact that she was a 'mum'!

The family stayed for a period of three years. During this time, realizing their need, I tried to give them presents and any articles of clothing (e.g. hockey jackets) that seemed appropriate. I would leave parcels at the door. Not once did Lena or either of my grandchildren ever thank me. I ignored their lack of manners and continued to give them all kinds of luxuries they could not afford.

One Christmas, I left a rather large parcel at the neighbour's house, with instructions to deliver the things to my daughter when she came home. Christmas came and went. My family was as silent as the grave. Finally, I went to the neighbour and asked whether the parcel had, in fact, been delivered, "Oh yes!" she said, "they got it all the next day!" I went over to the townhouse one Saturday afternoon to visit. Rui was home. I told him my mission. I was not going to provide any more goodies for the family, as they were so rude as to never even bother to say thanks. The children hung their heads. Rui exploded and asked Lena what was going on … after all, it had been a long stretch of time to "forget" to say thank you. Lena hung her head and was furious that she had been unmasked. Then came the time when the family achieved Canadian citizenship. It is normal for those who have helped the process along to be invited to the ceremony. I knew only accidentally that they had all become citizens. I had not been invited to attend the celebration!

There came a day when Rui was offered a very good job in Montreal. He decided to take it. It was one commensurate with his academic qualifications. (Later, he was offered jobs abroad once the children graduated from school. He and Lena travelled the world.) When I said goodbye to my grandsons, I chided them, saying that I would continue to give them presents but that, unless they were polite enough to thank me, no more would be forthcoming. It was their choice. They hung their heads, kissed me goodbye, and promised to write. To this day, forty years on, they never have sent me a letter. I learnt from my mistakes and stopped sending gifts on appropriate occasions. I have no idea what Lena told them, but they, in their wisdom, prefer to ignore me, even now as adults, when they should know better …

Lena is very status-conscious. Her house always has to be the biggest. It is always hard to have a serious conversation with her on any topic. She is content with external trappings.

My older grandson is a doctor and a surgeon, one who did very well in school and was an academic high achiever. My younger grandson is an economist. They all now live in Ottawa, including my daughter, who recently left British Columbia and sold the big house in West Vancouver. I did not know that she had gone to live in Ottawa. She did not bother to say goodbye (or even hello, for that matter, in all the time she stayed here).

I was quite surprised that she should move back to a region she hated because of its cold weather. I spoke to Rui on the phone, and he disclosed the reason they had moved. I learnt that I have a baby great-grandson (my grandson Johnny's child) who needs mothering. Rui even e-mailed me a picture of him. His name is David Alexander. I doubt that I will ever see him, but I wish him everything of the best.

My family seems to be together and thriving, and that is everything a great-great-grandmother can ever wish for!

*   *   *

When I retired, I decided that I would go overland with my trailer and stop in at Montreal to catch a glimpse of my family. I parked my trailer behind a small country church on the outskirts of Montreal and then drove off to visit the family I had not seen in ages. Lena opened the door. I was taken into the parlour and sat next to a Lena's friend Luz from Lisbon, who was visiting at the time. I was determined not to talk of controversial subjects. Luz and I spent several hours discussing the joys of doing cross-stitch (which I had never learnt and could not do). She was an expert in the area, and so the conversation stayed very neutral. We had quiche Lorraine for lunch. I was beginning to think that all was relatively peaceful when, surprisingly, Lena said that she decided to go to the mall. She went to change her clothes and then asked Luz to join her. To my surprise, they went out the front door. I was left alone in the house, sitting on the sofa, with only instructions to lock the door when I decided to leave…..

I must admit that I was caught off guard! Another interesting fact that I managed to find out is that when I asked Johnny, my youngest grandchild, why he never wrote to me, he, nearly in tears, said, "I did, I did, but Mummy put the postcards in the laundry always and forgot to post them."

I am hard-pressed to come up with some explanation for Lena's behaviour. But there are some things I know. She never wants to be "found out" by Rui, who has always been eminently fair in all his dealings. Rui, who was brought up in a military academy from the tender age of six (his father was a soldier) and had had no experience whatever of a mother figure in his life, is often mystified, given his rational mind, when perceiving traditional behaviour. Lena understands people's attitudes. She smiles an innocent smile of the "butter would not melt in her mouth" variety. Rui does not possess the emotional equipment to perceive fraud. He knows all about knobs and screws and electrical connections. He needs a course on human neurological wiring! He is kindly and, in fact, for all his degrees, is an innocent abroad. As he is a wonderful human being, I can only continue to wish him well. It will take him a lifetime to decipher the conundrum that is Lena!

THE JOY OF OWNING A FOREST

I had always had in the back of my mind the idea that living in the country would be a marvellous experience. I had always lived in cities but had felt a passion for wide-open spaces. I also felt that being in the midst of a dense forest was a mystical experience. The great silence, the slight tremors of the leaves in the wind, and the small sounds of the unseen life hiding in the foliage were magical.

I had long decided that the cost of land was prohibitive on the Canadian side of the border, but just below the 49th parallel, prices were quite reasonable. While wandering around the countryside one Sunday afternoon, Robyn and I stumbled on a five-acre parcel of land that was for sale. We made a foray onto the property and found that it was full of virgin-growth western cedars. From the northern boundary, it had clear views of Mount Rainier. I had found my forest.

On the way out through the underbrush, I stepped in a wasps' nest. We fled in a hurry, the wasps stinging all our exposed parts, and attempted to escape into the car, which was parked some distance away. The wasps had gone up the legs of my pants. In order to extricate them, I had whacked my limbs, with the result that I was severely stung. Robyn had some bad stings on his neck, and my legs were full of red welts. We were feeling a little sorry for ourselves. Despite this inauspicious beginning, I did buy the property the following week.

I had hoped to build a small house, but I finally settled on a rustic pole barn instead, for which I paid about ten thousand dollars. The barn contractor was the most sexist individual I have ever met. He was unable to make eye contact with me and kept deflecting answers to my son, who was, at the time, too young to be the main decision-maker. Robyn finally left the office, leaving me alone with the contractor. It was an uphill battle. The pole barn contractor talked to me as if I were the village idiot. While, at first, I was excruciatingly polite, I finally had to say to him that I was in full possession of my faculties and could understand what he was proposing. Would he mind addressing me directly in answering my questions? Was he aware that I was the one who was hiring him and paying his bills? He sat down and looked befuddled, but, slowly, we came around to signing a contract for the erection of a pole barn.

I was thrilled to see the building going up. I hired another contractor to put in a first floor under the slanted roofline. I had it clad in cedar. A very neat circular stairwell especially designed for the barn curled gracefully from the first floor to the second.

Over a period of two years, I completed an apartment under the eaves, put in a cedar-lined bathroom with huge glass windows which looked out under the cedars, and made a kitchen off the main living area. There was a large Lincoln wood-burning fireplace on a raised hearth.

I wanted to put in a well with water at fifty-seven feet and was delighted when the well contractor arrived and I found that it was a young woman in blue overalls who knew exactly what she was about.

I knew nothing at the time about sewers and wells and water heaters, but I had a great time researching all these things and then contracting to have them done. I even put on a large forty-foot veranda with stairs curling down into the forest. Sitting on this long veranda was wonderful because it raised me to the level of the main cedar tree branches, so it felt that I was, indeed, in the centre of a forest of green. It was a most satisfying feeling to build my own house. I had more fun living on the farm and building the upper-floor residential area than I have in all the places I have owned before or since.

When the house was nearing completion, I invited my daughter to come out and see the property and perhaps give me some ideas. She came under duress, but my grandchildren had a great time playing in the forest and collecting wild blueberries. I would sometimes collect my grandchildren on a Friday after my work and take them for the weekend. They would build imaginary tree houses, ride their bikes like cowboys, and sometimes even fall into nettle beds. I started a farm garden. The children planted their own patches with potatoes, rhubarb, and pole beans, and we devised ways to prevent the entry of rabbits and deer.

Much later, when Lena and Rui (respectively, my daughter and son-in-law) were posted to Adana in southern Turkey, I sent the grandchildren a Christmas cake and also included two small potatoes that had grown in Johnny's garden. These were duly delivered and cooked for him for lunch (and served with butter). He was thrilled to eat what he had planted.

At Christmastime, when the barn was completed, I sent out invitations for a family gathering on Christmas Day. I had presents for everyone. Although I am not a great admirer of this holiday and my family had always berated me for not making it a big production, I was, in this instance, prepared to be conventional. Tom said that he would come, and Robyn grudgingly said that he would, too ("I am not really a country boy" was his inane comment). The day before Christmas Eve, Lena phoned to say that she decided that she would rather stay in Vancouver, so neither she nor her husband, Rui (nor their children), would be coming for the family Christmas dinner where I had planned to show off the completed barn house.

I piled all the presents I had bought for the occasion into the car. I wrapped up the large frozen turkey and most of the food and took it to my daughter's house. She was not home, but I knew where to find her key, so I left everything I had brought on her kitchen table. I drove home and packed a suitcase. On Christmas Day, I left on a direct flight to Costa Rica.

I never mentioned the incident. In fact, as I gleaned from a conversation I had much later with Rui, I understood that he had had no clue about the Christmas invitation or that the turkey and the goodies had been my gift. I never spoke about it, and nobody ever mentioned it. It was the Christmas that never happened.

* * *

I occasionally had workmen over to help me with the cutting of downed trees. One rather unprepossessing individual, who had been recommended by a neighbour, rolled up one day. He had a long white beard and wore a dirty cap. His well-worn boots had metal caps. He seemed willing to work, was quite robust, and set about cutting wood with great gusto. He gave me his card, which read as follows:

Floyd B——

Sell or trade used cars, heavy equipment, whiskey stills, land, light bulbs, antiques, fish, guns, birds, wild reindeer, tools, caskets, native artefacts, bongos, clam and moose traps, gifts, hogs, hops, dogs, old airplanes, old coins, furniture, pots, pans, bells, souvenirs, horse collars, seashells, tombstones, confections, tricks, clothes, candy, turtles.

Underlined in bright orange ink was the following:

RUMOURS STOPPED, BARS EMPTIED, COMPUTERS VERIFIED, MANURE HAULED, TIGERS TAMED, FREE ADVICE.

WARS FOUGHT, RAVINGS QUELLED, GOVERNMENTS RUN, UPRISINGS QUELLED, ORGIES ORGANIZED, CONTRACTS CANCELLED.

I CAN FIX EVERYTHING FROM A BROKEN HEART TO THE BREAK OF DAY.

I laughed at the card, but, when I went inside the barn, I suddenly cried. It occurred to me that it would take this kind of man to fix my unfeeling family.

LOOKING BACK

Looking back, I judge myself as the luckiest of individuals. I have led a charmed life. My parents were wonderful people. I was loved and spoiled and given attention by a grandmother who considered it her job to look after me, love me, and cater to me from the moment I was born. I had no sibling to dilute her attention, and I was the happiest kid on the block. I developed a mature attitude to life quite early, and I knew how to entertain myself for hours. Very early, I became quite self-sufficient, and this has served me well in life.

Then there were the lucky accidents. So many people turned up at the right moments and turned my life into adventurous futures that I had never dreamed possible, ones which had led me to places and lives I had never thought possible, even in my moments of mad imaginings. Had I not formed a friendship with a girl called Yvette in my class at school, I would not have gone skating at the rink where, in a moment of madness, I crashed into a barrier and fell heavily onto the ice. I was picked up and helped by a tall, dark, handsome Canadian who had been innocently sipping coffee at the barrier. He helped rescue me from my fall. How could I have known that that meeting would alter not only the path of my life forever but also the future of my children and grandchildren forever?

I tried to plan my life carefully, and I worked hard at school as well as at university. I had ambitions and succeeded in attaining my goals. I was single-minded: I knew that I wanted to be totally independent, able to support myself financially, and that I wanted to see the world. I knew that I did not want to spend my time just looking after children, cooking, and cleaning house.

I realized that goals I set myself were difficult for a woman to attain. But the fact that my father had always told me that he had wished that I had been born a boy only spurred me further.

I was gifted with good genes, fairly good looks, a very healthy body, and intelligence, the last of which I had not realized I had until I was well into adulthood.

At the age of fifty, I still had time to hope, make drastic life changes, and even plan a new future direction, but at eighty, this is difficult. There are no longer the incandescent lights of a glittering future egging me onwards. There is only the dimming shine signalling the final forms of defeat.

This is the stage that is set for the final review of my existence. I have taken a detached look at my life in hindsight. Should I make any amends? Should I reverse hard stances that I had taken and felt strongly about? There is still a little time. There is the need to use time fruitfully. This I am doing to the best of my ability.

More recently, I have been teaching English to Iranian students and including a unit on Western culture, which, they all tell me, is a taboo subject in their country. I enjoy their company, and I like doing useful things. I have also recently discovered Panama City, Panama. I enjoy the tropics, the beaches, the people, and the fact that I am practicing my Spanish. I intend to go back there to sample Panama City's delights again this winter.

I spent my days in retirement travelling all over the world. I travelled extensively in Europe, Asia, Central and South America, and the Galapagos. I explored the forests of the Amazon as well as the far reaches of the Daintree Rainforest in Northern Queensland, and I have seen most of the islands of the barrier reef in Australia. I circumnavigated South America and saw the vessels bound for the Antarctic from the tip of South America in Ushuaia. I adored Thailand, lived in Japan and Singapore, and visited Kuala Lumpur and Indonesia. I had seen many countries in Africa, but I have not been back since I left so many years ago and I have no inclination to return. I took off in an Airstream trailer and circumnavigated the United States, which took me a year, and this trip provided more adventures than I had ever expected, and would probably make a book on its own. I also went back to Australia, rented a small apartment in Brisbane and stayed for a year at the Millenium. I would take off on the train to the North, visiting the glorious Northern Forests and spend weeks exploring the Barrier Reef where I stayed on various islands on the Reef itself to snorkel.

When I had, many years ago landed in Australia, I was considered "a very desirable asset" and the government in its wisdom sent me certificate of automatic citizenship in three weeks of arriving! I was stunned, as we had not even decided to stay at that time, and we were merely exploring the possibilities. I was surprised and flattered. I finally figured out why the Ozzies had done this. They are primarily interested in those English speaking individuals, from British Commonwealth Countries, (and similar culture)with certificates in areas where there is a need in Australia. I still have the certificate of Citizenship pegged to my wall. When I go back to visit, I always use my Ozzie passport, as this way I never have to get a visa, and I am always welcomed "home"! When I go the Europe I also go back as a "citizen returning" home with my Portuguese Passport signed by my Father, in such desperate circumstances, so long ago. It was late in life, when I arrived in Canada on my own that I was so surprised to get Canadian citizenship without ever applying for it, after just six weeks teaching at the College! I can only presume, and later verified, that the authorities had checked with the College, dug up my husband's papers as a veteran, saw that my Son was registered as Canadian at birth and sent me a Canadian Certificate of citizenship. I had never thought that I was such a "desirable" person........!! I as very touched by the gesture.

My eightieth birthday was one in which I spent the day utterly alone; not a single member of my family remembered it. But I have been looking over some of the events in my extraordinary life in which I have been terribly lucky. My life has been extraordinarily engaging, and I have had the luck of the Gods, who conspired to make my life very interesting, leading me to see amazing places. I have had deeply emotional experiences, been very healthy, and had a life that I largely embraced as one that I would have chosen anyway, had the Gods not conspired and had I been given the choice.